Saint Padre Pi

Prayers Meditations Reflections

James Mulligan

Published 2016 by Boanerges Press

Boanerges Press
616 Corporate Way
Valley Cottage
New York 10989
USA

ISBN-13: 978-1532815317

ISBN-10: 153281531X

Picture research James Mulligan

With grateful thanks to *www.padrepio.catholicwebservices.com*
and to *padrepiodevotions.org* for the use of material on the life of Saint Padre Pio

This book is intended for use as devotional material in the
Roman Catholic Parish of St Paul's, Harefield, Middlesex

Fr James Mulligan is Parish Priest of St Paul's Parish, Harefield in the Archdiocese of Westminster in London

In memoriam

Kristy Lear

30^h August 1991 - 15th May 2016

Saint Padre Pio ... A Brief Biography

Saint Padre Pio's official title is St Pio of Pietrelcina, but he will always be known as Padre Pio

Padre Pio (Francesco Forgione) was born to parents Giuseppa and Grazio Forgione in the small town of Pietrelcina, Italy on May 25, 1887. Although the Forgiones were poor in material goods, they were certainly rich in their faith life and in the love of God.

Even as a young boy, Francesco had already shown signs of extraordinary gifts of grace. At the age of five, he dedicated his life to God. From his early childhood, he showed a remarkable recollection of spirit and a love for the religious life. His mother described him as a quiet child who, from his earliest years, loved to go to church and to pray. As a young boy, he was able to see and communicate with, not only his guardian angel but also with Jesus and the Virgin Mary. In his simplicity, Francesco assumed everyone had the same experiences. Once a woman who noticed his spiritual demeanor asked him, "When did you consecrate your life to God? Was it at your first Holy Communion?" and he answered, "Always, daughter, always."

When Francesco was fifteen years old, he was admitted to the novitiate of the Capuchin Order of the Friars Minor in Morcone, Italy. He was admired by his fellow-students as well as by his Superiors for his exemplary behavior and his deep piety. One of the novices stated, "There was something which distinguished him from the other students. Whenever I saw him, he was always humble, recollected, and silent. What struck me most about Brother Pio was his love of prayer."

On August 10, 1910, at the age of twenty-three, Padre Pio was ordained to the priesthood. The celebration of the Holy Mass was for Padre Pio, the centre of his spirituality. Due to the long pauses of contemplative silence into which he entered at various parts of the Holy Sacrifice, his Mass could sometimes last several hours. Everything about him spoke of how intensely he was living the Passion of Christ. The parish priest in Pietrelcina called Padre Pio's Mass, "an incomprehensible mystery." When asked to shorten his Mass, Padre Pio replied, "God knows that I want to say Mass just like any other priest, but I cannot do it."

His parishioners were deeply impressed by his piety and one by one they began to come to him, seeking his counsel. For many, even a few moments in his presence, proved to be a life changing experience. As the years passed, pilgrims began to come to him by the thousands, from every corner of the world, drawn by the spiritual riches which flowed so freely from his extraordinary ministry. To his spiritual children he would say, "It seems to me as if Jesus has no other concern but the sanctification of your soul."

Padre Pio is understood above all else as a man of prayer. Before he was thirty years old he had already reached the summit of the spiritual life known as the "unitive way" of transforming union with God. He prayed almost continuously. His prayers were usually very simple. He loved to pray the Rosary and recommended it to others. To someone who asked him what legacy he wished to leave to his spiritual children, his brief reply was, "My child, the Rosary." He had a special mission to the souls in Purgatory and encouraged everyone to pray for them. He used to say, "We must empty Purgatory with our prayers." Father Agostino Daniele, his confessor, director, and beloved friend said, "One admires in Padre Pio, his habitual union with God. When he speaks or is spoken to, we are aware that his heart and mind are not distracted from the thought and sentiment of God."

Padre Pio suffered from poor health his entire life, once saying that his health had been declining from the time he was nine years old. After his ordination to the priesthood, he remained in his hometown of Pietrelcina and was separated from his religious community for more than five years due to his precarious health. Although the cause of his prolonged and debilitating illnesses remained a mystery to his doctors, Padre Pio did not become discouraged. He offered all of his bodily sufferings to God as a sacrifice, for the conversion of souls. He experienced many spiritual sufferings as well. "I am fully convinced that my illness is due to a special permission of God," he said.

Shortly after his ordination, he wrote a letter to his spiritual director, Father Benedetto Nardella, in which he asked permission to offer his life as a victim for sinners. He wrote, "For a long time I have felt in myself a need to offer myself to the Lord as a victim for poor sinners and for the souls in Purgatory. This desire has been growing continually in my heart so that it has now become what I would call a strong passion. . . It seems to me that Jesus wants this." The marks of the stigmata, the wounds of Christ, appeared on Padre Pio's body, on Friday, September 20, 1918, while he was praying before a crucifix and making his thanksgiving after Mass. He was thirty-one years old and became the first stigmatized priest in the history of the Church. With resignation and serenity, he bore the painful wounds in his hands, feet, and side for fifty years.

In addition, God endowed Padre Pio with many extraordinary spiritual gifts and charisms including the gift of healing, bilocation, prophecy, miracles, discernment of spirits, the ability to abstain beyond man's natural powers from both sleep and nourishment, the ability to read hearts, the gift of tongues (the ability to speak and understand languages that he had never studied), the gift of conversions, the grace to see angelic beings in form, and the fragrance which emanated from his wounds and which frequently announced his invisible presence. When a friend once questioned him about these charisms, Padre Pio said, "You know, they are a mystery to me, too." Although he received more than his share of spiritual gifts, he never sought them, never felt worthy of them. He never put the gifts before the Giver. He always remained humble, constantly at the disposal of Almighty God.

His day began at 2:30 a.m. when he would rise to begin his prayers and to make his preparation for Mass. He was able to carry on a busy apostolate with only a few hours of sleep each night and an amount of food that was so small (300-400 calories a day) that his fellow priests stated that it was not enough food even to keep a small child alive. Between Mass and confessions, his workday lasted 19 hours. He very rarely left the monastery and never took even a day's vacation from his grueling schedule in 51 years. He never read a newspaper or listened to the radio. He cautioned his spiritual children against watching television.

In his monastery in San Giovanni Rotondo, he lived the Franciscan spirit of poverty with detachment from self, from possessions, and from comforts. He always had a great love for the virtue of chastity, and his behavior was modest in all situations and with all people. In his lifetime, Padre Pio reconciled thousands of men and women back to their faith.

The prayer groups that Padre Pio established have now spread throughout the world. He gave a new spirit to hospitals by founding one which he called "The Home for the Relief of Suffering." He saw the image of Christ in the poor, the suffering, and the sick and gave himself particularly to them. He once said, "Bring God to all those who are sick. This will help them more than any other remedy."

Serene and well prepared, he surrendered to Sister Death on September 23, 1968 at the age of eighty-one. He died as he had lived, with his Rosary in his hands. His last words were Gesú, Maria – Jesus, Mary – which he repeated over and over until he breathed his last. He had often declared, "After my death I will do more. My real mission will begin after my death."

In 1971, Pope Paul VI, speaking to the superiors of the Capuchin order, said of Padre Pio, "What fame he had. How many followers from around the world. Why? Was it because he was a philosopher, a scholar, or because he had means at his disposal? No, it was because he said Mass humbly, heard confessions from morning until night and was a marked representative of the stigmata of Our Lord. He was truly a man of prayer and suffering."

In one of the largest liturgies in the Vatican's history, Pope John Paul II canonized Padre Pio on June 16, 2002. During his homily, Pope John Paul recalled how, in 1947, as a young priest he journeyed from Poland to make his confession to Padre Pio. "Prayer and charity–this is the most concrete synthesis of Padre Pio's teaching," the Pope said.

Drawing approximately eight million pilgrims each year, San Giovanni Rotondo, where St. Pio lived and is now buried, is second only to the shrine of Our Lady of Guadalupe in Mexico in its number of annual visitors.

St. Pio's whole life might be summed up in the words of St. Paul to the Colossians, "Now I rejoice in my sufferings for your sake, and in my flesh I complete what is lacking in Christ's afflictions for the sake of his body, that is, the Church."

St. Padre Pio pray for us.

The young Padre Pio with the stigmata

Prayer for the Intercession of St. Pio of Pietrelcina

Dear God, You generously blessed Your servant,
St. Pio of Pietrelcina,
with the gifts of the Spirit.
You marked his body with the five wounds
of Christ Crucified, as a powerful witness
to the saving Passion and Death of Your Son.
Endowed with the gift of discernment,
St. Pio labored endlessly in the confessional
for the salvation of souls.
With reverence and intense devotion
in the celebration of Mass,
he invited countless men and women
to a greater union with Jesus Christ
in the Sacrament of the Holy Eucharist.

Through the intercession of St. Pio of Pietrelcina,
I confidently beseech You to grant me
the grace of (here state your petition).

Glory be to the Father... (three times). Amen.

Stay with me, Lord

Prayer of St. Pio of Pietrelcina after Holy Communion

Stay with me, Lord, for it is necessary to have
You present so that I do not forget You.
You know how easily I abandon You.

Stay with me, Lord, because I am weak
and I need Your strength,
that I may not fall so often.

Stay with me, Lord, for You are my life,
and without You, I am without fervor.

Stay with me, Lord, for You are my light,
and without You, I am in darkness.

Stay with me, Lord, to show me Your will.

Stay with me, Lord, so that I hear Your voice
and follow You.

Stay with me, Lord, for I desire to love You
very much, and always be in Your company.

Stay with me, Lord, if You wish me to be faithful to You.

Stay with me, Lord, for as poor as my soul is,
I want it to be a place of consolation for You, a nest of love.

Stay with me, Jesus, for it is getting late and the day is coming to a close, and life passes;
death, judgment, eternity approaches. It is necessary to renew my strength,
so that I will not stop along the way and for that, I need You.
It is getting late and death approaches,
I fear the darkness, the temptations, the dryness, the cross, the sorrows.
O how I need You, my Jesus, in this night of exile!

Stay with me tonight, Jesus, in life with all its dangers. I need You.

Let me recognize You as Your disciples did at the breaking of the bread,
so that the Eucharistic Communion be the Light which disperses the darkness,
the force which sustains me, the unique joy of my heart.

Stay with me, Lord, because at the hour of my death, I want to remain united to You,
if not by communion, at least by grace and love.

Stay with me, Jesus, I do not ask for divine consolation, because I do not merit it,
but the gift of Your Presence, oh yes, I ask this of You!

Stay with me, Lord, for it is You alone I look for, Your Love, Your Grace, Your Will, Your Heart,
Your Spirit, because I love You and ask no other reward but to love You more and more.

With a firm love, I will love You with all my heart while on earth
and continue to love You perfectly during all eternity. Amen.

Visit to the Most Blessed Sacrament

Padre Pio recited this prayer daily. It was written by St. Alphonsus Liguori.

My Lord Jesus Christ, for the love which You bear to men, You remain night and day in this Sacrament full of compassion and of love, awaiting, calling, and welcoming all who come to visit You. I believe that You are present in the Sacrament of the Altar: I adore You from the abyss of my nothingness, and I thank You for all the graces which You have bestowed upon me and in particular for having given me Yourself in this Sacrament, for having given me your holy Mother Mary for my advocate, and for having called me to visit You in this chapel. I now salute Your most loving Heart: and this for three ends:

1. In thanksgiving for this great gift;

2. To make amends to You for all the outrages which You receive in this Sacrament from all Your enemies;

3. I intend by this visit to adore You in all the places on earth in which You are the least revered and the most abandoned.

My Jesus, I love You with all my heart. I grieve for having so many times offended Your infinite goodness. I promise with Your grace never more to offend You in the future. Now, miserable and unworthy though I be, I consecrate myself to You without reserve; I give You my entire will, my affections, my desires, and all that I possess. From now on dispose of me and of all that I have as You please. All that I ask of You and desire is Your holy love, final perseverance, and the perfect accomplishment of Your will. I recommend to You the souls in purgatory; but especially those who had the greatest devotion to the most Blessed Sacrament and to the Blessed Virgin Mary. I also recommend to You all poor sinners.

My dear Saviour, I unite all my affections with the affections of Your most loving Heart; and I offer them, thus united, to Your eternal Father, and beseech Him in Your name to vouchsafe, for Your love, to accept them.

Amen.

A Prayer for Trust and Confidence in God's Mercy

by St. Pio of Pietrelcina

O Lord, we ask for a boundless confidence and trust in Your divine mercy, and the courage to accept the crosses and sufferings which bring immense goodness to our souls and that of Your Church. Help us to love You with a pure and contrite heart, and to humble ourselves beneath Your cross, as we climb the mountain of holiness, carrying our cross that leads to heavenly glory. May we receive You with great faith and love in Holy Communion, and allow You to act in us as You desire for your greater glory. O Jesus, most adorable Heart and eternal fountain of Divine Love, may our prayer find favour before the Divine Majesty of Your heavenly Father.

Efficacious Novena to the Sacred Heart of Jesus

Padre Pio recited this novena every day for all those who requested his prayers

I. O my Jesus, you have said: "Truly I say to you, ask and you will receive, seek and you will find, knock and it will be opened to you." Behold I knock, I seek and ask for the grace of...... *(here name your request)* Our Father....Hail Mary....Glory Be to the Father....**Sacred Heart of Jesus, I place all my trust in you.**

II. O my Jesus, you have said: "Truly I say to you, if you ask anything of the Father in my name, he will give it to you." Behold, in your name, I ask the Father for the grace of.......*(here name your request)* Our Father...Hail Mary....Glory Be To the Father....**Sacred Heart of Jesus, I place all my trust in you.**

III. O my Jesus, you have said: "Truly I say to you, heaven and earth will pass away but my words will not pass away." Encouraged by your infallible words I now ask for the grace of.....*(here name your request)* Our Father....Hail Mary....Glory Be to the Father...**Sacred Heart of Jesus, I place all my trust in you.**

O **Sacred Heart of Jesus**, for whom it is impossible not to have compassion on the afflicted, have pity on us miserable sinners and grant us the grace which we ask of you, through the Sorrowful and Immaculate Heart of Mary, your tender Mother and ours.
Say the Hail, Holy Queen and add: St. Joseph, foster father of Jesus, pray for us.

St. Margaret Mary Alacoque

Padre Pio Testimonials

You think you know my love for you but you don't know that it is much greater than you can imagine. I follow you with my prayers, with my suffering and with my tears.

– St. Pio of Pietrelcina

Drinking Problem

Late one night walking to my home from work, I was praying the Rosary for help to overcome a problem I had with alcohol, which was worsening. I was newly married, had an infant son and I realized that unless my drinking problem was defeated my future would be filled with disaster. I was determined to overcome the problem and in my worry about it, I turned to Padre Pio for help as I prayed the Rosary. Suddenly I became aware of a fragrance of indescribable character. It seemed to envelop me with its delightful aroma, which produced a deep sense of peace and satisfaction. Suddenly the fragrance stopped. A few steps later I was home and as was my practice, the first thing I did, was to visit my infant son asleep in his crib. As I entered my son's room, again, the fragrance returned. Then it vanished. Remember, I had asked Padre Pio to help me overcome my alcohol problem. Quite amazingly I must tell you, from the night of the fragrance to this very day, I developed and have maintained a deep disgust for alcohol, and for more than twenty years have had no desire whatsoever to drink alcohol in any form. It was after this experience that I learned that Padre Pio often uses fragrances as a sign that a prayer will be answered. – Name Withheld

My Prayer Was Taken to Padre Pio's Tomb

I had a dear childhood friend, Timothy, who had been homeless for five years after struggling with addiction and depression. He had no family and his whereabouts was unknown to all of his former friends, including myself. I was able to send a written prayer petition concerning Timothy with another friend who was visiting the tomb of Padre Pio in San Giovanni Rotondo. Out of millions of homeless people, my old friend, Timothy was chosen to be helped in a special way by a non-profit organization that works to rehabilitate those who are addicted and in great need. They raised a lot of money for him, sent him to rehab, and found distant family members that he never knew he had. His relatives then took him in to their home. He now lives near them, has a job and an apartment. He is happy with his new life. The odds of this happening and of me finding out about it stagger all comprehension and I give all glory to all powerful and all loving God, Father, Son, and Holy Spirit, through the intercession of Padre Pio. – Jim Stewart

Healed in a Dream

After suffering for ten years, in December, 1983, I started the novena to Padre Pio. In February, my condition grew worse. My ankles became swollen and the pain was unbearable. On February 10th, I was healed in a dream. I was in a beautiful chapel and Padre Pio came to me. He told me to sit and then he touched my swollen ankles. He touched my back and then he said, "Get up and walk. You are healed." I awoke immediately from my bed and I walked without a single pain in my body. That morning I attended Mass to thank our Lord. The pain came back, but only for a moment because soon what felt like a warm hand touched my back and took my pain away. I have never known that pain again. – Gregory William Collins

Consolation Through Padre Pio's Intercession

I lost my only son very tragically last year. I was very troubled as to whether my son was happy in his new dwelling. I prayed faithfully and daily to Padre Pio for some sign from my son. One night my son came to me in a dream and told me that God was very just and that he, my son, was happier than he had ever been on earth. I feel that this was more than a dream. – M. Feeney

Healing from Cancer

We were asked to pray a novena to Padre Pio for a 13 year old lad who was dying from progressive malignant cancer in the lower abdomen. The sick child, Michael Andrews, had a tumor the size of a baseball sitting on his left pelvis and it could be clearly seen and felt as a large swelling. One night, Michael's mother heard him shouting and screaming in pain. She rushed to his room but when she got there she found him sound asleep. She was mystified. Something made her look behind at the Padre Pio picture in his bedroom. All the white areas in the picture were glowing in the dark. In order to ensure that it was not some light creeping in, she closed all the doors. However, the picture of Padre Pio continued to glow. She ran her fingers over the glowing areas. They were real enough. After a little while the visitation went away and all fell into darkness. Next morning Michael found that the large tumor so prominent in his lower abdomen had disappeared. When taken back to the hospital, the doctor could find nothing. – M. Shaw

Mental Anxiety

I would like to share with you the grace I received from Padre Pio. In October of 1987, I was very depressed and nearly had a nervous breakdown. Because of this mental state, my thoughts were very threatening and very, very frightful. In my darkest moment, my mother introduced me to Padre Pio and told me he would help. From that day onward I put all my trust and faith in Padre Pio and prayed to him daily for a cure for my state of mind. Then one night, I awoke suddenly and saw the figure of a monk in a brown robe with a beard. The next morning I told my mother of this experience. She told me it was Padre Pio watching over me. From that night onward I began to feel better. Today I feel great and I am a dedicated follower of Padre Pio. – Pasquale Presta

Father John brought Padre Pio's Glove to Children's Hospital

My daughter Elizabeth was 8 years old when she was diagnosed with Hodgkins disease, a type of cancer. She stayed at Our Lady's Children's Hospital in Dublin for a number of weeks. I used to visit her on my lunch break from work every day and also at the end of my work day before going home. Her throat was affected by the disease and she lost the ability to speak. One day a nun, who was the head nurse on my daughter's ward, pulled me aside to speak to me privately. She did not want my wife to overhear our conversation as she said that my wife seemed to be a very emotional person. She told me that Elizabeth was not going to survive the cancer. After she told me that, I went to the Capuchin Friary at St. Mary of the Angels in Dublin. One of the Capuchin's, Father John, had a glove of Padre Pio's. I asked him to visit Elizabeth and bless her with it. I have had a devotion to Padre Pio for many years. I have also attended daily Mass for almost 50 years, since the year of my marriage in 1960. Father John came to the hospital and blessed Elizabeth with the glove as well as all of the other children who were there. Not long after, I was having a meal at the Fish and Chips restaurant on Kimmage Road in Dublin. Suddenly, the whole area was pervaded with the fragrance of roses. I instantly knew it was Padre Pio. I also thought to myself that it was an odd place for him to make his presence known. A few days later, I spoke to the head nurse again. She told me that she had astounding news for me – all of Elizabeth's tests were normal. My daughter recovered rapidly and completely and her voice came back full strength. When she got older, she sang professionally throughout Europe. I believe that through the intercession of Padre Pio, my daughter was healed. – Michael Gormley

Nervous Breakdown

I made a novena to Padre Pio about four weeks ago for my brother. For the last seven years he has been homebound after having a nervous breakdown. He had been on medication and seeing a psychiatrist on a regular basis. Instead of getting better he was getting worse. He stopped going out completely. We were all concerned for him as he is only 34 years old and living the life of a recluse while being dependent on my elderly parents. I made the novena as suggested. One day after the novena (my mother did not know that I made this novena) my mother informed me that my brother had actually gone out on his own for a walk and then a few days later he went for a drive with my mother. This was a giant step from how he was before. His doctor is very impressed with his improvement and has cut back his medication. He is now going for walks on his own. He is actually driving alone now and even talking of trying to seek employment. This is truly a miracle. – Name Withheld

My Mother-in-Law was Healed

I am from Cebu City, Philippines. One day when I passed by Cebu Cathedral Church, I noticed a great crowd of people were there for the Mass. When I went inside, I saw that a picture of Padre Pio surrounded by beautiful flowers had been placed on the altar. I asked someone what the occasion was and I was told that it was a Mass in honor of Padre Pio because he was going to be canonized soon. I stayed for the Mass and ever since that time I have had a devotion to Padre Pio. I pray to him every day and I pray to him like a father. My wife and I have felt his blessings in our life. In October of 2004, my mother-in-law, Josefina

DeLira (Mama Fe) was taken to the Perpetual Succor Hospital in Cebu City. The ultra sound revealed that she had kidney stones and would have to have surgery to remove them. When my wife, Liza Joy and I got to the hospital, we brought Mama Fe a little icon of St. Pio. Mama Fe was very scared about having the surgery. We told her not to worry about anything. The truth is that my wife and I were very worried about her condition and were also worried because we did not have the money to pay for the operation or for any of the other medical expenses. Mama Fe has no medical insurance. We did not want her to know of our fears and so for her peace of mind, we told her we could handle the doctor bills even though we did not know how we would be able to. We told her not to worry about anything but to put all her trust in St. Pio. She said that she would. Early the next morning, Mama Fe suffered a tremendous pain in her stomach. It was so severe that she could not even cry out for a nurse to come and assist her. She reached for the icon of St. Pio and placed it on her abdomen and prayed for him to help her. Then she fell into a deep sleep. She woke up to find the doctor at her bedside, examining her. A test revealed that all of the kidney stones had disappeared. The doctor was so surprised. He could not believe what had happened. No surgery was necessary and Mama Fe was then released from the hospital. I know that this healing was brought about through the intercession of St. Pio, who is very close to God, Jesus and Mother Mary. Thank you St. Pio for everything. – Celestino Petallar

Healing from Terminal Cancer

Luigi Antonelli, the playwright, went to the doctor and cancer was found covering the area between his ear and his shoulder. The doctors told him that with surgery, he would be able to live for six more months but without it, he only had three months to live. He would have undergone the operation immediately, had not one of his friends advised him to go to San Giovanni Rotondo and see Padre Pio. Luigi agreed and attended Padre Pio's Mass and afterward went to confession. What happened during this confession? Antonelli found it difficult to describe even though he was a man who had a way with words. During confession he had a long conversation with Padre Pio and the longer it went on, the more his soul was transported into a celestial state. At the same time he felt a kind of current circulating in his body, eradicating all traces of the cancer. When he got off his knees, Antonelli felt in good health. His soul, as well as his body, had been cured. He took up all his activities without ever experiencing again the slightest symptoms of cancer.

Healing from Alcoholism

I am an alcoholic and had to be hospitalized due to alcohol poisoning. All of the doctors concerned pronounced me a vegetable. The brain damage was so severe, the doctors said there was no hope of recovery. With the best medical care and attention, there was no hope at all. Some person, of whom I do not know to this day, left a picture of Padre Pio beside my bed and it was from then on that I began to get better. I am now completely and fully healed with no sign of brain damage. I am also a recovered alcoholic and have been for many years. – Name Withheld

Pray for the Souls in Purgatory

In 1964, I travelled from the Philippines to San Giovanni Rotondo with my parents and siblings to visit Padre Pio. However, we were unable to see him because he was ill at the time and we left San Giovanni disappointed and with heavy hearts. But on June 7, 2006, I was able to go there once again on pilgrimage. I was able to view his relics and see his home and church. I saw the brand new modern looking basilica that has been erected in his honor. But it is to the older church of Our Lady of Grace that I was drawn. There I felt the presence of Padre Pio very strongly. In the old church I knelt beside Padre Pio's confessional and prayed to him and made a general confession. I tried to recall the many, many sins of my life and I humbly asked his intercession for God's pardon. Then, in my heart, I felt Padre Pio talking to me. I felt that he was asking me to say one Our Father, one Hail Mary, and one Glory Be, for the souls in Purgatory, everyday for the rest of my life. Afterwards, I went to the bookstore inside the church. There I saw a book with Padre Pio's picture on the cover titled, "The Holy Souls." I purchased the book and learned that Padre Pio offered his Masses, prayers and sufferings for the release of the Holy Souls who are in Purgatory. I had no knowledge of this before I read the book. I feel that my prayer was heard by Padre Pio and that he truly spoke to me in my heart. Padre Pio truly lives. Viva Padre Pio! – Carmelino P. Alvendia Jr.

Depression Lifted

Over the past twenty five years, I have suffered on and off from severe endogenous depression. However, last year I experienced the worst bout I had ever had. It began in December 1991 and lasted continuously until October 1992. During all of this time every possible medication and treatment were tried but nothing seemed to work. I felt miserable. I could not eat or sleep or do any housework. I lost a lot of weight and there were days when I did not even feel able to wash or change my clothes. Most of the time I felt unable to go to Mass, but used to watch it on TV or listen to it on the radio. I prayed constantly to Padre Pio. In October my husband and I went on a pilgrimage to San Giovanni Rotondo. It was a wonderful experience to pray at his tomb. On our last day there I awoke to the beautiful smell of incense. I felt really good and the depression had lifted for the first time in almost a year. Since then the depression has not returned. It is all thanks to Padre Pio. – Mary Maher

Healed from Sadness

My dear husband died suddenly. He was 45 years old. My children had both moved away so I was left in a big house on my own. Most nights, I would go to bed and cry, even scream hysterically while pleading with Jesus and his mother to help me. I had two nervous breakdowns. I was invited to a showing of a Padre Pio film and I was moved deeply. I was blessed with Padre Pio's mitten. One night, as I was dreading the thought of going to bed, I felt the presence of Padre Pio all around me. From that time onward, I have never really had a bad night. – Name Withheld

Safety in Time of War

My brother was serving in the army and had been sent to Viet Nam. Every night our family prayed for his safe return. I carried Padre Pio's photo with me and prayed to him often for my brother. I felt Padre Pio's presence with me and shortly after that, my brother wrote to say he would be coming home. When he did come home, he was a different person. After that terrible war he became more quiet and serious. We never asked questions about his experiences and he never spoke much about it. He did mention one experience which seemed very peculiar to him. He said that one day his company was sent ahead of the others to check for the Vietcong. They were looking through the bush with their guns, when suddenly all of the soldiers smelled the fragrance of roses. They kept saying "Where are the rose bushes? It sure smells good out here." They never did find the rosebushes and were sent back to camp. Another company was sent out to inspect the same territory. How tragic to say that the company was ambushed and not one survived the attack. According to the calculations, the Vietcong had been there lurking in the bush all along, when my brother and the others in his company were in that area. But for some strange reason, they were not attacked and they very easily could have been. I know it was Padre Pio who saved my brother's life. – I. Ahmadzai

Confidence Regained

I had not been out of my house for 25 years and I had not seen my dear brother in all those years. He found my address from my sister and she told him about my problem. I had never heard of Padre Pio but I had a dream about him. In my dream he smiled at me. Also one day, I noticed the beautiful fragrance of flowers in my living room although there were none in the house. Finally, I got the courage to go to church one day. I bought a magazine there and found out about Padre Pio. My dear brother came to see me after 25 years and he told me that he had been praying to Padre Pio for me to regain my confidence. – Name Withheld

My Uncle's Whole Life Changed

In the 1920's and 30's, my father and some of my uncles who lived in Texas got involved in trafficking illegal liquor from Mexico to the U.S. side of the border. They would then sell the illegal liquor in the U.S. My uncle, Eleno Rojas, got caught and was sentenced to 3 to 4 years in jail and served his time in El Paso, Texas. Being in that jail was a frightening experience. Terrible crimes were committed there, not only by the inmates but also by the jailers. My uncle feared for his life and wondered whether he would survive in that terrible jail. Uncle Eleno had learned about Padre Pio through his parents. At the time, Padre Pio was a young priest. My uncle prayed all the time that God would protect him. One night as he was praying, his cell became filled with a beautiful fragrance of roses. He felt a great sense of peace. He saw Padre Pio standing in front of him. Padre Pio communicated to Uncle Eleno that everything would be all right. Shortly after that experience, my uncle was released from jail. He never failed to thank Padre Pio for coming to his aide and for the rest of his life he would talk about Padre Pio to anyone who would listen. He often spoke of, "the miracle that happened in his cell." Uncle Eleno's whole life changed after that experience with Padre Pio and it changed the lives of the rest of the family as well. We all became very devoted to Padre Pio. All of my uncles left their former lifestyle behind them and they all became successful merchants. My uncle Eleno passed away in 2006. He was 100 years old. Isn't it strange that I work at Central Jail in Los Angeles and I see what many inmates go through. I see their fear and loneliness. I used to see them wearing their rosaries until a rule was made that no longer allowed it. I would tell the prisoners, "Don't just wear it around your neck, pray the Rosary as well." I see that for many who are incarcerated, the only thing that can sustain them is their faith. – Hortencia Perez

Entrust Everything to the Child Jesus

During Advent of 1952, I approached Padre Pio for confession, during which I strongly recommended my neighbor to him and asked him to pray for her. Padre Pio then gave me a beautiful little picture of the Infant Jesus of Prague, telling me that Christmas time was particularly suitable for asking for graces. Then, blessing the picture, he advised me to entrust everything to the Child Jesus. – Katharina Tangari

A New Person

A close friend of mine has made a complete transformation through the intercession of Padre Pio. She told me that in spite of friends and money, no one had ever made her truly happy. She tried to heal the emptiness of her life by the heavy use of drugs and alcohol. Failed relationships and all the trappings of a fast life brought her nothing but loneliness. She made attempts to take her own life. Once when she was very high on drugs, she jumped out of a window and broke her leg very badly. One day as I was driving her to the doctor's office, she noticed for the first time, the rosary of Padre Pio hanging on my car mirror.

She asked about it and held it, saying it was pretty, so I told her about Padre Pio. With great interest she held the rosary so I told her to keep it and to pray. The acceptance of the rosary was the beginning of her healing. She quit alcohol and drugs and became a daily communicant and a catechism teacher every Sunday at her parish. For someone who had not gone to church for twenty five years, this was a big leap for the love of God. We look at her now and feel as though we are looking at a new person. – Lupe Abad

Padre Pio's Medal

My older brother, the father of two beautiful twin girls had been a very heavy drinker and drug abuser for years. He did not see his family or his children towards the end of his addiction, in fact he was living in a tent with homeless people just a few miles from my parents' home. I prayed and prayed that my brother might find his way and have a good life. I would try to speak about God and Our Lady and give him Padre Pio prayer cards, all to no avail. However, my prayers were answered and a few months ago, my brother was saved from his hell on earth. He entered a rehabilitation clinic for drugs and alcohol and has joined a support group for his addictions. He has a new job now and is living with my parents. He sees his beautiful daughters every week. Just the other day, I looked at his jacket and I saw that our beloved Padre Pio's medal was attached to the zipper. I know that Padre Pio has helped him and is giving him strength. – Bridget Walsh

Padre Pio said, "Never Offend the Lord again."

In January 1961, Nando Umile made a trip to San Giovanni Rotondo and was able to make his confession to Padre Pio. At that time, the confessions were held in what was commonly referred to as the "old sacristy" of the church of Our Lady of Grace. One of the Capuchins was always present to show the pilgrims the proper procedures and to maintain order. He allowed the men to enter the dimly-lit sacristy, ten at a time. They sat together on a bench as they waited their turn. The sacristy was divided in half by a curtain and Padre Pio heard confessions from behind the curtain while the penitent knelt beside him. When Nando entered the confessional, Padre Pio asked him in a calm and serious voice how long it had been since his last confession. After Nando answered, Padre Pio asked him to confess his sins. At the conclusion of his confession, something quite amazing happened. In Nando's own words: "I had hardly finished my confession when a bright light descended in rays upon Padre Pio. This light was strange in that it only lit up the body of Padre Pio without spreading even a centimeter beyond him. All the rest of the sacristy remained in semi-darkness. The light that surrounded Padre Pio lasted for about 30 seconds. As I stared at Padre Pio, I realized that he had had a vision." Nando observed that during those sacred moments, Padre Pio's face had suddenly become bright red. When the light disappeared, Padre Pio seemed startled and as if awakening from a dream, he said to Nando, "Who are you and where do you come from?" Nando replied that he lived in Rome. Padre Pio then said in a gentle voice, "You come from

Rome. Well, let me advise you to never offend the Lord again." With that, he gave Nando a final blessing and said the parting words, "Now go in peace."

An Extraordinary Blessing

My boyfriend Joe became addicted to methamphetamine. After endless attempts to get help for him, I told him that the relationship was over unless he agreed to get into a rehabilitation facility. He entered a rehabilitation program on Thursday, February 9, 2006. The next day he decided that he didn't need help and left the facility. I felt that the next time that I would see him would probably be at his funeral. After crying most of the night, the next morning I looked at my mail and saw an envelope from the Capuchin Franciscan Friars. I usually toss them in the trash, but instead I opened it and inside was a prayer card and a picture of St. Pio of Pietrelcina. The words of St. Pio said, "Pray, hope, and don't worry. Worry is useless. God is merciful and will hear your prayer. Prayer is the best weapon we possess. It is the key that opens the heart of God." I had never seen a picture of St. Pio before. I knew that I needed to pray for his intercession. I called Joe and told him that I was very disappointed that he gave up so easily and left the rehab facility but that I was going to help him in a way that I hadn't tried before. I hung up the phone and I prayed. Later that evening Joe called me. He told me that he had not given the rehab facility a chance and that he had called the counselor at the facility (on Saturday) and asked if he could reenter the program. He was told that he would have to wait for a vacant room. On Monday, Joe called me to say that he spoke to the program director who said that he had never had a patient leave and then call and beg for another chance. The director said that they would have an empty bed on Wednesday and that if Joe wanted it, he needed to be there by 9:30 a.m. or it would be given to someone else. I was skeptical because Joe was not a morning person and was never on time for anything. Joe was able to reenter the facility on Wednesday. He called me on Sunday. Joe, the man that I had never seen cry, sobbed uncontrollably. He said that he had gone to Mass that day. He told me he was so sorry that he always gave me such a hard time when I would beg him to go to church with me. He said that he realized now that his addiction was something that he couldn't fix by himself and he now knew how critical it was that he get help. Joe finished the program and was discharged. He has faithfully followed up with outpatient care and attends Narcotics Anonymous meetings weekly. He has not missed Sunday Mass or Holy Day Mass since. I pray daily to St. Pio to continue to heal Joe and to keep him strong in his recovery. Recently, we took a weekend trip to the beach with my family. While sitting in the back of the church at Sunday Mass, Joe leaned over and whispered, "St. Pio is watching us." I looked up to find an enormous picture of St. Pio on the wall directly beside us. Thank you St. Pio for giving Joe his life back. – Karen Merritt

My Life was Only an Existence

I was a broken man, a wreck, and my life was only an existence. My brother Christopher, sent me the prayer card of Padre Pio asking me to entrust all my troubles to him and that relief would come soon. I started to recite the prayer daily. Words cannot express my relief. – Theophilus Weldt

It was Not Certain if I Would Live Through the Night

I learned about Padre Pio through a newsletter called "Pray, Hope, and Don't Worry" which I found in the church vestibule at Good Shepherd parish in San Diego. I attend the Mother of Perpetual Help Novena at my parish and one Tuesday night at the Novena, when I looked at the picture of Our Mother of Perpetual Help, I seemed to see Padre Pio looking at me. In February 2006, I had a hemmorhagic stoke after having a heated argument with my sister. I was lying unconscious on the floor when paramedics came and rushed me to the hospital. The right side of my brain was bleeding and the left side of my body was paralyzed. It was uncertain whether I would live through the night. I remained in a coma for three weeks in the Intensive Care Unit. The neurosurgeons told my family to look for a nursing home for me because even if I came out of the coma I would be nothing but a vegetable. I did come out of the coma and I was able to walk and to speak with no difficulty. During my hospitalization I could always feel the presence of Padre Pio and Mother Mary with me. – Danilo Ganzon

Padre Pio said, "Go Home at Once!"

Paulette Bertels of Antwerp, Belgium was able to make a trip to San Giovanni Rotondo in 1965. She had to be back in Antwerp by December 25 because she was scheduled to conduct the Cathedral Choir at the Christmas Mass that year. She did not want to leave San Giovanni Rotondo until it was absolutely necessary because every moment near Padre Pio was precious to her. On December 22, to Paulette's great surprise, Padre Pio said to her, "Go home!" She protested saying, "But Padre I wanted to stay here as long as possible. I still have time to be here a little longer before going back to Belgium." He replied, "Go home at once!" There was nothing for Paulette to do but obey him. Paulette took a taxi to Foggia and when she got to the railway station, the station master asked her where she was going. "I am going to Milan on my way home to Belgium," she said. He answered her and said, "You are very lucky. This is the last train that will be leaving for Milan before the railway strike." If she had not been on that train, she would not have made it home in time for the Christmas Mass. Who knows how the choir would have managed without their conductor. Paulette then remembered how insistent Padre Pio had been when he told her to return to her home and she was very grateful.

The Miracle Twins

My daughter was expecting her first baby and from the beginning, things were going wrong. After some time, tests revealed that she was carrying twins, yet there was only one heartbeat. The doctors did not think the babies would survive. They also said that the babies might have to be taken prematurely. I wrote a letter to Padre Pio and he said that he would pray for my daughter. The babies were both born alive and healthy. Her doctors called them the "miracle twins." – Winifred Robison

He Was Not Expected to Live Until Morning

Capuchin Brother Christopher, OFM, Cap., was one of Padre Pio's spiritual sons. On one occasion, when Brother Christopher was admitted as a patient to Sydney Hospital in Australia, he had the opportunity to witness a miraculous healing through the intercession of Padre Pio. There in Sydney Hospital, a young man about twenty years of age occupied a bed in the same ward that Brother Christopher was in. The young man had a good job as a clerical worker at the headquarters of the Peter's Ice Cream Factory in Redfern, Sidney. Brother Christopher learned that he had been in the hospital for quite some time. The young man's condition mystified the medical staff. His temperature use to rise to abnormal degrees, so much so that the nurses had to pack his body in ice in order to reduce his fever. He was unable to hold down any food. The young man's condition deteriorated rapidly after Brother Christopher's first ten days in the hospital. One night around midnight, the young man's family and girlfriend were summoned to the hospital because his end was near. Since he was a Catholic, the Catholic chaplain from St. Mary's Cathedral, Father Edmund Campion, was called. After visiting the young man, Father Campion came to Brother Christopher's bedside and said to him, "Please pray for this young man who is in your ward. He is leaving us tonight. He is not expected to last until morning." Brother Christopher promised Father Campion that he would do so. After Father Campion left, Brother Christopher remembered that he had a picture of Padre Pio with him which he had received from San Giovanni Rotondo. He had read of many accounts of miracles that had occurred when Padre Pio's picture was placed under the pillow of a sick person. He gave the picture to the young man's family and told them about the holy life of Padre Pio. They thanked Brother Christopher and said they would place the picture under his pillow. At seven o'clock the next morning, there were startled looks on the faces of the nurses and doctors when they saw that the young man appeared to be strong and healthy. He was able to sit up in his bed and he ate all the food on his tray. He then got http://padrepiodevotions.org/wp-admin/users.phpout of bed and came over to Brother Christopher and spoke to him for the first time. "I want to thank you for the picture of Padre Pio," he said. "I feel sure that it saved my life." The young man was released from the hospital several days later, completely cured. Before leaving, he and his girlfriend came over to Brother Christopher's bedside to thank him once again. They promised that they would return to the hospital soon to visit him. But before they were able to do so, Brother Christopher was also released from the hospital.

Saved From A Serious Accident

I credit Padre Pio with bringing me back to the faith, after having learned of him in the mid 1970's. He made it possible for me to believe what before I could not believe. I thought that the Bible and all of the stories of Catholic saints were just fairy tales. But after looking at Padre Pio's life, I could no longer hold that view. Recently I was mowing my lawn. I was walking backwards, finishing the last strip. What I didn't realize was that I was about to walk backwards into a large support beam on my children's swing set while pulling the running lawn mower. In the instant before I would have walked backwards into the swing set, Padre Pio popped into my head and said, "I'm right behind you." This caused me to pause. With my very next step I felt my heel come against the post that I was about to collide with. I have no doubt that I would have fallen, pulling the lawnmower over my feet and lower legs. I wasn't thinking about or praying to Padre Pio at the time that he popped into my head. This leads me to believe that I received special protection. I praise God for giving us Padre Pio. He has helped those like me who could not believe, to believe! And I praise God and I thank Padre Pio for saving me from this accident. – Joe Fusco

I Felt as if a Great Burden Had Been Lifted

I recently went to the Catholic women's prayer breakfast, the Magnificat. The talk that was given was on Padre Pio. After the talk, some of the relics of Padre Pio were there for veneration. I touched my Rosary to the relics and as I did so I felt a kind of jolt in my body. I felt very light as if a great burden had been lifted off of me. At the same time I thought of my mother. My mother was very much into the occult. She was always trying to get me involved in it too but I refused. Even so, I have always felt this hanging over me. All of my life I've looked for ways to be rid of this feeling but to no avail. When I touched the relic of Padre Pio, I felt at last that I was released from the darkness that I often felt around me. I feel totally renewed. My friend who was with me said, "Look how your Rosary is shining." I looked at it then and the crystals were indeed shining. The silver too looked different. It looked brand new. The Rosary had been given to me by my mother more than fifty years ago. Thank you, God. – Elva Eastman

While Watching a Film on Padre Pio

My daughter, while watching a Padre Pio film show in our church hall, was suddenly relieved of a throat condition that had troubled her for several years. I was with her at the time and seemed to feel that something had happened to her. When we were leaving the hall, she appeared to be in a mild state of shock and she said to me, "It's gone, mom. The lump has gone from my throat." The next day she told what had happened more fully and that her throat condition was cured. That was four years ago, and she has indeed been cured. – Mrs. C. France

My Father was Close to Death

My father, Michael DeMaria, is greatly devoted to Padre Pio. His own father, my grandfather, had gone to confession to Padre Pio in the late 1940's. When he went into the confessional, Padre Pio greeted him by his first name, John. My grandfather asked him how he knew his name and he told him simply that he knew many things. Padre Pio also told my grandfather that he would have a very good life in America and his words proved to be true. Things went very well for my grandfather when he moved to America. My father had a very serious fall which caused bleeding in his brain. He was close to death. He was taken to the hospital in Akron, Ohio, and had brain surgery. My mother was told by the doctors to get all of his affairs in order because he was not expected to live. When I visited him in the intensive care unit of the hospital, his kidneys were failing and besides the brain surgery, he had many other serious health problems and complications too numerous to mention. I printed out some testimonials about people who were gravely ill who had been healed through the intercession of Padre Pio. I taped them to the wall in the hospital beside my father's bed. That was when my father told me that Padre Pio had come to him and stood beside his bed and prayed for him. Padre Pio assured him that he would be all right. He said that Padre Pio spoke to him in English. My father even described the brown robe that he was wearing. My father was in intensive care for many weeks and in the hospital for a total of six months. That was three years ago. In 2006, my father celebrated his 81st birthday. Our family knows, without the intercession of Padre Pio, my dad would not be here. When we visited the Padre Pio shrine in Pennsylvania, my father had an opportunity to hold Padre Pio's glove. As he looked around at the grounds of the shrine, my father softly said, "This must be what Heaven is like." – Denise DeMaria Bowman

A Priest Remembers Padre Pio

I am a Catholic priest and years ago I accompanied a sick man to San Giovanni Rotondo, who hoped to be cured by Padre Pio. I was happy to have this opportunity to see Padre Pio. The sick man whom I accompanied was not cured and I smelled no perfumes. Moreover, when I went to confession, Padre Pio did not lift any mysterious veil from my soul. For me, he was only a good confessor, like many others. Yet I did see something. For many days, I heard Padre Pio say Mass and for me that was everything. I heard Mass from the side of the altar and I did not miss a single gesture or expression. I had already said thousands of Masses, but in those moments I felt that I was a poor priest, the same way I felt during confession. Padre Pio really spoke to God in every moment of the Mass. I could even say that he struggled with God, like Abraham. And God was present. Thus at San Giovanni Rotondo I found a priest who loved God truly and intensely, in suffering and prayer, even to agony; a real saint.

My Son Came to See Me from Heaven

My son Frankie was diagnosed with Osteosarcoma (bone cancer) in July of 2005. He fought a long and hard battle against this illness for twenty seven months. He had four lung surgeries, amputation of his leg, radiation, and countless rounds of chemotherapy. He also developed a secondary cancer, leukemia. During his ordeal, Frankie, kept hopeful and prayerful. He kept Jesus as the center of his life, and prayed to his patron saint, Padre Pio, whose picture he always kept with him. Frankie died on Sept. 14, 2007. He was 17 years old. The morning of Frankie's Mass of Christian Burial, my family and I were at the funeral home where there had been a public viewing of Frankie for two days. When it was almost time to say goodbye to my son and go to St. Ephrem's in Brooklyn for the funeral Mass, I felt my strength failing me. I dreaded this final time, knowing I would never see my son again. At that moment I prayed to Padre Pio, begging him to help me. The moment I finished my prayer, into the funeral home walked Ray Ewen. Ray had met Padre Pio in 1945 when he served in the U.S. military and was sent overseas to Italy. Ray has been a great promoter of Padre Pio ever since. Ray prayed for my son and he prayed for me. As he prayed, I felt a great sense of peace come over me and I received the strength I needed so badly. I know that Ray's presence was an answer to my prayer. Ray does not live close by but he told me that when he woke up that morning he felt a very strong urge to get to the funeral home and see Frankie. It was not easy for him but he managed to find a ride with a close friend who was also very devoted to Padre Pio. The celebrant of Frankie's funeral Mass was Father Gerard Sauer. He was joined by four others priests and over 1000 people attended. Two beautiful eulogies were said, one by Frankie's best friend, Gennaro Anzalone and the other by Dr. Joseph Marino, the Principal of Frankie's school, Xaverian High School in Brooklyn. Dr. Marino told all present about Frankie's faith in God and his devotion to Padre Pio. It wasn't long afterward that I had a vivid dream about my son. In my dream, Frankie looked well and he was breathing easily. I thought that he was alive again. He let me know that he was in Heaven and only back to speak to me for a moment. He told me that he was in a place that was so beautiful that it was impossible to describe. He also told me he was with other children. I asked him if Padre Pio was there. Frankie looked at me and said, "Padre Pio was there to meet me when I arrived." – Camille Loccisano

Testimony of an Eyewitness

I visited the friary of Our Lady of Grace in San Giovanni Rotondo and attended Padre Pio's Mass. I asked one of the seminary students at the monastery to show me Padre Pio's cell. The boy kindly lead me to it. Standing in front of his cell, I was struck by a breeze that had a delicious and continuous perfume which gave me such spiritual joy that I did not want to leave. I called other people who were nearby and they all experienced the same phenomenon. To be more certain, I repeated the experiment with the doors of other cells but I smelled no perfume. At confession as well as during Padre Pio's Mass, one had the impression of being in the presence of someone who is not of this world. A great force of sanctity emanated from his whole person and it carried away those present, filling them with holy thoughts and devout contemplation. – Gennaro Cascavilla

Padre Pio Guided My Little Sister to the Next World

My thirteen year old sister Bernadette was paralyzed from birth. She was very bright and very pretty. In the last year of her life she suffered great sickness and severe pain with very little sleep or rest. She always wore a relic of Padre Pio pinned to her vest. One morning, Bernadette told us that she had slept all night and that a lovely man appeared at her bedside during the night. She said he wore a long dress with a rope tied around the waist and he had a beard. He told her he was taking her away to a land where she would have no pain or sickness ever again. Upon hearing this, my mother became very upset. The man held her hand and she said she was not afraid because he was a holy man. Bernadette asked him to leave her here a little bit longer. She talked about the "holy man" all the time. As the days went by we all knew she had seen somebody because she seemed so peaceful. Six weeks later, on June 1, 1978 Bernadette died with no pain. Padre Pio appeared to my little sister and took away her fear of death and guided her gently from this world to the next. – Elizabeth Reid

Padre Pio Hears Our Prayers

A poor widow woman from Bologna, with five children had visited Padre Pio. She asked him to accept her as one of his spiritual children. She also asked him to keep all of her children in his prayers. He heard her confession and after the meeting, she prayed to Padre Pio every day. In her prayers, she asked him to watch over her children, protect and bless them. Five years later she visited Padre Pio again and during confession she asked him to watch over her children. He said to her, "How many times do you intend to ask me that question?" She told him she did not understand. He replied, "You have asked that of me every day for the last five years!"

Healing Dream

In July of 1992, I was diagnosed with lymphoma. I went through 6 months of chemotherapy. One night my son asked me if I had ever heard of Padre Pio and he told me a little bit about him from a program he had seen on television. My son is not very religious but was quite taken with this man at the time. Sometime shortly after this I had a dream. In my dream I was out walking alone and saw a group of people. I made my way toward them. As I approached, the others seemed to vanish and the back of this man, whom I thought was Jesus, drew me closer. As I went to speak, the man turned around. At first I saw his gentle face and then his eyes. Rays shot from his eyes and went through me. I woke up. My friend gave me a prayer card of Padre Pio. Imagine my surprise when I looked and saw that it was the man in my dream. I told my friend of my dream and she saw it as a sign of healing from my cancer. I've thought of that ever since. I just finished my first year of tests and the cancer shows no signs of recurrence. – Pat Yanics

Peace of Mind

While serving a short prison sentence, a friend sent me a novena to Padre Pio. I discovered from that day on that I was given great peace of mind, and I believe that Padre Pio has helped me in many ways and still does to this day. – Name Withheld

I Had No More Pain

I had to have a very serious operation in which one of my kidneys was removed. As a result, I nearly died. After spending many weeks in the hospital, my doctor finally let me come home. My grandfather, who has already passed away, was deeply devoted to Padre Pio. I felt that I had come through the surgery by prayer and by faith. However, I was unable to walk, feed myself or do anything for myself. My mother was taking care of me and I was dependent on her for everything. The pain and discomfort that I felt was almost unbearable and because of it, I had to take diamorphine several times a day. One day a neighbor came to the door. She asked my mother if she could see me. When she came in my bedroom I was surprised because I did not know her very well. I did know that she had a strong faith. She took a small box out of her bag and in it was a glove. She told me that it was Padre Pio's glove. She pressed the glove against my side on the area where I had the operation. I do not know the circumstances of how my neighbor came into possession of Padre Pio's glove. All I know is that from the moment she touched me with it, I had no more pain. I could walk and sit up. I was still weak but from that day forward I began to feel stronger. This experience has changed my life. – Caroline Millar

He went to Mass and Holy Communion

My husband Jerry was a lapsed Catholic, so I put the leaflet with the third class relic of Padre Pio in his pillow case. He did not know he was lying on it. Jerry's birthday was the 23rd of September, so I put one of the same leaflets in his birthday card. I prayed to Padre Pio, "Please bring my husband back to confession." Three days later, when I was getting ready to go to bed, I said good night to Jerry and he said to me, "You know Lorna, I went to confession today and I also got on a bus and went to Mass and received Holy Communion." Praise God and thanks to Padre Pio. – Lorna Smyth

A Blessed Rosary

I met Padre Pio during World War II, when I was stationed in Cerignola, not far from San Giovanni Rotondo. I was able to attend Padre Pio's Mass and even visit with him in the garden of the monastery, where he would sometimes have his lunch. Meeting Padre Pio was a blessing that has remained with me my entire life. When I returned home to New York after the war was over, I used every opportunity to tell others about Padre Pio. I have been a parishioner at the Sacred Heart parish in Queens for more than sixty years. A number of years ago, our pastor's sister, who was a Dominican nun, asked me if she could borrow the Rosary that I have, which was blessed by Padre Pio. I agreed and she took it to where she worked at Mary Immaculate Hospital in Jamaica, New York. Later, when she returned it, she told me that one of the patients in the hospital heard about the Rosary and asked her if he could pray with it. He was healed for when he went into surgery to have a cancerous tumor removed, it had disappeared. – Ray Ewen

My Brother Met Padre Pio During World War II

My brother Bill was drafted into the U.S. Air Force and served as a tail gunner during World War II. He flew 50 missions over Germany. During that time he was stationed in Foggia, Italy where the Americans had an air base. On one occasion, Bill traveled to San Giovanni Rotondo with one of his Air Force buddies in order to attend Padre Pio's Mass. During the Mass, Bill witnessed the stigmata, the wounds Padre Pio suffered. On another occasion, the pilot that Bill crewed with, asked him to accompany him on a visit to see Padre Pio. They hitchhiked part of the way and then walked the rest of the way up the hill to the monastery. Bill felt very fortunate to be able to have a private audience with Pare Pio. An interpreter was there to help them with the language barrier. Bill introduced the pilot to Padre Pio. "You have been here before," Padre Pio said to him. "No, this is my first time coming here," the pilot replied. Padre Pio then said that on a certain date, shortly after midnight, he had flown his plane directly over the monastery. The pilot had no distinct recollection of that particular date and gave Bill a puzzled look. However, Padre Pio had made quite an impression on him. When they got back to the base, the pilot immediately went to his log book and looked up the date that Padre Pio had spoken of. Indeed, he realized to his amazement, that he would have been flying over the monastery at the very time that Padre Pio had mentioned. On Christmas Eve of 1945, my family was gathered at my parent's house in West Lynn, Massachusetts. My mother looked out the window and there was Bill walking up the street toward our house. We had no idea that he was coming home and we were overjoyed at his safe return. On that very night, he told us the story of meeting Padre Pio, a story I have never forgotten. – Marguerite Manning Shea

On Heroin

I was down and out and homeless. I was a heroin addict. I wanted to kick the habit on my own, but I couldn't do it. I had no money nor medical insurance. The city hospital had a long waiting list and no other help for me was available. My aunt and her friends started praying to Padre Pio for me. At first I didn't believe, but then everything started going o.k. for me. I was admitted into a hospital for detoxification and then I was sent to an excellent rehabilitation program for drug addicts. I am now working and off drugs and trying to rebuild my life. Thanks be to God and Padre Pio's powerful intercession. – Name Withheld

Harassment

I had a terrible problem with a young man harassing me and calling me names. Eventually it got so bad that even his family started to threaten me and my husband. I prayed to Padre Pio to help me. I am happy to say I have all faith in his intercession. The man phoned to apologize after I had prayed to Padre Pio just once. – Name Withheld

A Blessing

I am of Cajun descent and I speak both English and some Cajun, although broken Cajun. My daddy died on December 8, 1990. However, on December 7th, at St. Mary's Hospital in Port Arthur, Texas, while staying near daddy's bedside, my husband and I witnessed daddy seeing someone come in to his room. My daddy's eyes followed them to his bedside and he extended his hand and was very serious and very humbled by whoever it was that he saw and he commenced to speak to them. We knew that there was someone very holy and very powerful there and that also there was more than one person near him. The language my daddy was speaking is one I had not heard until this morning when my husband and I were listening to a recording of Padre Pio's voice. I recognized it as the language my daddy was speaking. It was either that language or something very close to it. We just knew that there were some very holy people escorting him into eternal life. I have never seen my daddy become so humbled as he was that day. He died the next morning. I knew we were in the company of holiness, of saintliness and we were not hung out to dry. They were powerful and they knew God. I have known about Padre Pio for many years and I am wondering if it might have been Padre Pio who was there at my daddy's bedside. What is hard for me is to see that I am worthy of Padre Pio coming to my aide and to my families' aide. Thank you, Amen. – Mary Ellen Breaux Weisse

My Father Never Touched Alcohol Again

I had a wonderful and devoted father. I loved him very much. He was a very good man, well known for his generosity. Nothing would stop him from helping anyone in need or in trouble. However, he was completely indifferent to all religions, especially the Catholic Church, though he professed to have a vague sort of belief in God. On top of that, he had serious drinking problem. He used to drink heavily almost day and my mother joined him in his drinking. All my persuasions and remonstrations did not seem to have any effect and I was in deep despair over it. It was at this time, 1962, that an uncle told me about Padre Pio and his work. I wrote to Padre Pio and asked him to pray for my parents so that they would be converted and give up drinking. Unexpectedly, after some time I got a letter assuring me that Padre Pio was praying for my parents. In 1977 my parents became interested in the Catholic faith, took instructions, and were baptized. However, it took my father another six years to give up drinking, which he finally did in 1978. He never touched alcohol again after that. – Mary Therese Man Lu Cing

My Doctor said, "What Have You Done"

About 20 years ago I attended a seminar given by a priest who had returned from a trip to San Giovanni Rotondo. His testimony about Padre Pio was very inspiring and since that time I have developed a very close relationship with Padre Pio. I keep a small Padre Pio prayer card in the left pocket of my shirt at all times. Every night I place it on my night table before I go to bed. I obtained a Master's Degree in Theology and Pastoral Ministry from Barry University and I am also a Certified Public Accountant. My wife and I have been active parishioners at St. Timothy Catholic Church in Miami where we head the Evangelization Ministry. I also teach Bible classes on Tuesdays. In 2010, I was diagnosed with severe aorta stenosis. My aorta valve should have had an opening of 3 cms. and mine showed only .75. To confirm the findings, my cardiologist, Dr. Hugo Garcia ordered a transesophageal echo test. The test showed the same results. My doctor explained to me that I was going to have to have open heart surgery. I met the doctor who was going to perform the surgery, Dr. Nirberto Moreno, at Baptist Hospital of Miami. When he saw the results of the echo test, he characterized the aorta stenosis as "critical." Before the surgery, I had to have one other procedure, a heart catheterization. The procedure would take a close look at my arteries in order to determine the entry point for the open heart surgery. It my arteries were in good shape, the surgeon would go through the side of my chest. If the coronary arteries were obstructed, the center of my chest would have to be opened for the surgery. The heart catheterization procedure was performed at South Miami Hospital on April 12, 2011. As I was coming out of the sedation, my cardiologist, Dr. Garcia, said to me, "Mr. Contreras, what have you done?" I did not understand what he meant and was afraid that he had bad news for me. "I have not done anything. But I have prayed a lot," I replied. "Well, keep praying," my doctor said. "Your aorta valve now shows a 1.44 cm. opening. You do not need heart surgery." I had been praying to Padre Pio since January, asking only that my coronary arteries would be healthy. Well, Padre Pio went all the way for me!" –Jorge Contreras

Healing from a Lifelong Illness

During my childhood I was afflicted with an illness from the age of 8 years old. I could not attend school very much but I was able to take piano lessons. Every week I had a private lesson in my home. Doctors told me I would have the illness all my life. I met Padre Eusebio (Padre Pio's secretary) when he visited Ireland and he told me about Padre Pio. He said he would talk to Padre Pio about me when he returned to San Giovanni. Padre Pio advised that I have pupils and teach them piano. I made a trip to San Giovanni and I met Padre Pio in 1966. He told me I would have to suffer for 3 years and then I would be cured. I am now completely cured and have my own school where I teach piano in my home and have 40 pupils. I am getting on well thanks to Padre Pio. – Mary Kennedy

I Thank Padre Pio from the Bottom of my Heart

I would like to give thanks to Padre Pio who has interceded for me throughout my life. I graduated from Sheffield Hallam University in Yorkshire in the north of England in 1983. At that time, I lived in a rented room above a bookshop and was far away from home, as I am from Scotland. The bookshop had a lot of Marxist, anarchist, feminist, and communistic books. I had access to all the reading material and I had read a lot of Marx and Freud. I looked to science and reason rather than faith to explain human existence. I considered myself an atheist and a marxist. The bookshop also had a variety of other kinds of secular reading material and had a contract to supply the city library with books. One night while browsing through the stacks, I came across John McCaffrey's, 'Tales of Padre Pio.' I read the book at one sitting and was deeply impressed. The next morning I received a letter from my mother containing a Padre Pio prayer card and relic. It was at a time in my life when I was scared and uncertain of the future. I decided to make the prayer novena to Padre Pio to ask for guidance in my life. As a result, I won a scholarship to study for a post-graduate degree in Glasgow, Scotland. Padre Pio has been my protector and benefactor ever since and has never failed me even in my darkest times. I love and thank him from the bottom of my heart for helping me to reaffirm the beauty and peace of my Catholic faith. Viva Padre Pio! – Kenny Keegan

My Daughter was Delirious

About a year ago, my oldest daughter, Debbie, age five, began having terrible nightmares. She would dream that people were shooting her or tying her up. She would wake up in a delirious state and scream, not recognizing me or my husband or even know where she was. I tried blessing her bed and room with holy water every night but nothing seemed to help. My husband had attended a presentation on Padre Pio here in Milwaukee and obtained one of his relics. With faith in the sanctity of Padre Pio, we placed his relic under my daughter's pillow. She never had another nightmare again. – Mrs. Richard Boldin

Testimony of Padre Agostino

Padre Agostino, Padre Pio's Spiritual Director, left this recollection: Padre Pio suffered and prayed for all and in a special way for the Vicar of Jesus Christ. Very often the Lord sends spiritual and bodily sufferings for the salvation and the good of souls. Padre Pio once told me that he had suffered for a particular individual for almost two months. He said to me, "I don't know the reason for this, but I suffer." When I was getting ready to leave for Genoa for the hospital, I stopped to see Padre Pio and he was in bed. He told me, "My Father, go in peace, because you have someone who is praying and suffering for you." I answered, "Let's divide the suffering." He replied, "Don't give it another thought." All went well with me at the hospital and all thanks are due to Padre Pio who suffered and prayed.

A Marriage Renewed

My husband was treating me terribly. I could not take this mistreatment any longer. I begged Padre Pio to help me. I had no where to go for help but Heaven. One evening I was already in bed and the room was very quiet when my husband went to his side of the bed. He was lying down about five minutes when he suddenly jerked his head up and in a shocked voice said to me, "Someone has just whispered in my ear, 'Love your wife.'" My husband changed after that experience and became much nicer to me. We have three children now and attend Mass together as a family every Sunday. – Name Withheld

From Seoul, South Korea – Amazing Grace

Some time ago, one of my American friends gave me a photo of Padre Pio. I was grateful for his gesture but I didn't really believe what he said to me about Padre Pio. But I kept the photo in my Bible anyway. Also, another friend sent me a Christmas gift which included a book on Padre Pio. Even though I flipped through the pages, I still found it hard to believe, so I just put this book on the shelf and I forgot about Padre Pio. Last year (2013) in the summer, while I was sitting in the Mapo Library in Seoul, I was reading one of the testimonies on the Padre Pio website (padrepiodevotions.org) just out of curiosity. And while I was reading, there was one story which really struck me because the story seemed so much like my sister's situation. It was the story of a thirty-four year old man who had a nervous breakdown and had stopped going out of the house and was living the life of a recluse. My sister was in a terrible situation because she had been unable to find work for many years and was often ill and depressed. She frequently refused to go out of the house, was not meeting or seeing people, and she cried a lot. We were very worried about her and also exhausted after trying in many different ways to help her, and nothing had worked. So, after I read the testimony, I decided to pray to Padre Pio. There in the library, I prayed sincerely and with my whole my heart to Padre Pio, asking for his help. And then I started to smell a really clear and fresh flower scent of violets! The windows were all closed in the library and the air conditioner was running, so I was really perplexed. It was very, very strange. There was no place that the beautiful, fresh scent of flowers could possibly come from. I realized then that Padre Pio was going to help my sister. And then I prayed and waited. Within two months, my sister found that she was eligible to enroll in a good education program which teaches Information Technology skills to those who are unemployed. She is no longer depressed and devastated as she was before. She has been meeting people from her class and she no longer cries. She doesn't refuse to go outside anymore. I was really surprised to see all the changes that happened so fast. The dramatic change in her life style in general was simply remarkable to me. And I want to say many thanks to Our Father in Heaven who listened to our agony and of course to Padre Pio for his generous help even though I didn't trust him for years. – Name Withheld

Sent a Telegram to Padre Pio

I had just come out of the hospital with a severe nervous disorder, near a nervous breakdown. I had been working at a bank near my home where I was a credit collection correspondent for delinquent mortgages. This work where I had to collect money on delinquent mortgages from poor, desperate and sick people finally undermined my health until I was admitted to the hospital for six weeks. When I returned from the hospital, my recovery didn't seem to be forthcoming. In desperation one day a sent a telegram to Padre Pio and asked for his intercession. That night my sister and I were in her apartment. My sister knowing nothing about the telegram exclaimed, "What is that gorgeous fragrance? Do you smell it?" At first, I couldn't understand the significance. Then it dawned on me where this heavenly fragrance came from. That much I did know, that when Padre Pio was interceding for you, he would let you know by a fragrance. My healing did not come at once but from then on the whole course of my life started to change for the better. By January of the following year there was a complete break from the past. I can look back to that period as a turning point in my whole life. – Name Withheld

He was Always Praying

The following testimony is from Padre Federico who was one of Padre Pio's seminary students. Padre Pio also acted as his spiritual director. Padre Pio was always praying, night and day. His main teaching place for us was the choir, where he spent long hours of the day on his knees as a faithful worshiper of Jesus in the Blessed Sacrament. In our midst he prayed and responded, always holding his Rosary in his right hand. In the refectory, after having hurriedly and listlessly swallowed a few mouthfuls, he continued to pray. He used to say "I wish the day had forty-eight hours in which to pray." In fact, he never left the choir until midnight. When he went to bed we felt him to be always keeping watch. His whole day was a continuous dialogue with God. – Padre Federico of Macchia Valforte

Padre Pio Rescued Me in Vienna

mental illness. In 2008, in the middle of a personal crisis, my husband left home. I felt into a deep depression and was unable to find a way to get out of the gloom and sadness that had engulfed my life. I had to make a business trip to Vienna which I could in no way postpone. I did not want to make the trip and was in no shape to be alone in a foreign city. I found strength in prayer and the Eucharist. When my Rosary broke, I went to a shop to buy a new one. A gentleman in the shop gave me a prayer card, with a third class relic of a saint that I had never heard of, St. Pio. The prayer card had the Novena to the Sacred Heart of Jesus and the prayer for the intercession of St. Pio. I prayed the Novena and the prayer for St. Pio's intercession every day, and I slowly started feeling better. I went to my mother's house for the holidays. One night, my mother and I were watching T.V. As she was changing the channels, I told her to stop on one particular channel. "That man looks like the saint on the prayer card I was given in Vienna," I said to my mother. I went to get the prayer card to look at it closer. The television program was a movie about the life of Padre Pio. The next day, I went to a Catholic bookstore and bought a book on Padre Pio. I found out that his feast day is September 23, the day of my wedding anniversary. My husband came back home and is now taking care of his illness. Today is our 15th wedding anniversary. I am very thankful to St. Pio because I know he made it possible for me to accept what I have to live with and for my husband to return home and take care of his illness. I tell people that St. Pio rescued me. He found me in Vienna, there is no doubt about it. He reached out through that gentleman who gave me the prayer card. He touched my life and my heart and brought me closer to Jesus. We know the road is not easy, but I have confidence that I have Padre Pio's help to walk as Jesus would want me to walk. Every night I pray to St. Pio for all the people I know who are sick, including my husband. – Name Withheld

Padre Pio Had a Halo Like the Saints

I made a trip to San Giovanni Rotondo on June 29, 1968, just three months before Padre Pio passed away. My time there was very brief. The church was so crowded for his Mass that I was unable to find a seat. I had to stand for the entire Mass. Even so, I was able to see Padre Pio well. At the end of the Mass, he left the altar accompanied by his fellow friars. I did not take my eyes off him for a moment until he disappeared into the sacristy. He was very beautiful. He had a halo like the saints. I had only one thought "This is the grace of communion with God." An hour later, I began my journey home. I happened to speak with a spiritual son of Padre Pio who had also been at the Mass. I told him of my impressions and asked him if he too had seen a halo surrounding Padre Pio's head. He said that he had not. When the news of Padre Pio's death came on September 23, 1968 I thought, "This is the end of his suffering." In my mind, I saw his beautiful radiant smile again as he would appear before God. – Laura Dell' Andrino

Conversion

I went to the hospital to give Holy Communion to one of the patients there. As I was about to leave, the Sister who worked at the hospital said to me, "The man in the end bed is a Catholic. Please go and see him." When I saw the man I said to him, "I believe that you are a Catholic" and he replied, "I used to be a Catholic many years ago, but I have not been to church since I don't know when." We spoke awhile and before I left I gave him a relic card of Padre Pio and asked him to read it when he felt like it. He took the leaflet from me and just placed it on his bedside with little interest in it. Some days later I went to the hospital again to make my rounds. The man who I had taken Holy Communion to said to me, "The man in the end bed wants to see you. He has been asking when you were coming in." I went to the man and he invited me to take a seat. He said, "I have made every provision for my business and my family, but as I read the little history about your friend Padre Pio, I began to realize that I forgot about my own situation. Is it possible that I could make my confession to an understanding priest? I do not want to be interrogated." I told him that I knew a very gentle priest. The priest came right away. In the meantime the man's wife, son and daughter came to visit him and when they saw the curtain pulled round the bed they thought the worst until they saw the priest pulling the curtain back. His wife said to us that she had never seen her husband looking so relaxed and happy since he came to the hospital. The man showed the relic card of Padre Pio to his family and he said to me, "Please give my wife one of the lovely leaflets of Padre Pio." Three days later he died a very peaceful and happy death. May he rest in peace. – Peter Barrett

I Received a Hand-Written Note from Padre Pio

I am a native of Czechoslovakia and as a six-year-old lad, I heard our Lord's call to be a priest. It was a great grace to receive such an invitation. Yet early in life I realized the impossibility of studying theology in Czechoslovakia, so when I was about 13 years old I wrote to Padre Pio, "Padre, please help me to become a priest and if I cannot study at home, please help me to get abroad." I received a hand written note that Padre Pio was praying for me. In 1976, as an immigrant, I arrived in Canada where I began my studies required for ordination and on August 25, 1989, by the grace of God and through the intercession of our Blessed Mother and Padre Pio, I was ordained a priest. I am very, very happy to be a priest and to belong to the Church which has so many, many saints in every age but especially in our own time. Padre Pio, thank you! – Father Paul Hancko

The Waitress Told Me How Tough Her Life Was

Once, when my daughter and I were having dinner at one of our favorite restaurants, the Country Squire Diner in Broomall, Pennsylvania I got into a conversation with our waitress. She told me how tough her life was. She was a single parent and was in need of a place for her and her young son to live. She was down to the wire where she was living and needed help fast. She worked long hours at the diner trying to save her money for a decent place to live. I asked her if she had ever heard of Padre Pio and she said that she had not. I wrote his name down and told her to read about him online and then to pray to him for help. About five months later I returned to the restaurant. "Oh thank God you are here," I heard the waitress say as I walked in the diner. She then gave me a hug and said to me, "I have been hoping you would return because I want to share my miracle of Padre Pio with you!" The waitress told me that after reading about Padre Pio she prayed to him as I had suggested. After she had saved enough money, she began to look for a small house to rent. Her mother allowed her and her son to move in with her until she found a place. She found one place that she liked very much but when she found out the rent was $2000.00 a month she became sad. "I am sorry I bothered you," she said to the owner of the home. "I didn't realize the rent was so expensive. I cannot afford it. I have prayed so hard to Padre Pio to help me." "How do you know about Padre Pio?" the owner of the house asked. Then she explained how I came to the restaurant and talked to her about Padre Pio. The owner asked her how much she could afford for rent and she told her that $700.00 a month was her limit. "Then that is the price it will be, because any friend of Padre Pio is a friend of mine!" the owner said to her. – Patti Karlton

Sister Pia D'Apolito

Sister Pia D'Apolito, who was born and raised in San Giovanni Rotondo, had contact with Padre Pio on several occasions during her youth. She was just fifteen years old when she met Padre Pio for the first time. She described him as being "very kind and very handsome, with gentle manners, even though he could be severe on occasion." He was thirty years old at the time. Like all of the other citizens of San Giovanni Rotondo, Sister Pia and her family were very much aware of Padre Pio's reputation of holiness. They were also acquainted with his parents, Grazio and Giuseppa Forgione. Sister Pia never forgot the time Grazio and Giuseppa paid a visit to their home. They were very worried about Padre Pio's exhausting schedule at the monastery and said, "Our poor son, they are going to kill him by making him stay so long in the confessional!" They were also deeply concerned about his deteriorating health but felt at a loss to know what to do to help him. Sister Pia's brother, Brother Giovanni Crisostomo, was one of the Capuchin students who lived at the monastery of Our Lady of Grace. In order to assist him in meeting his financial obligations, the superior of the monastery made a special arrangement. In exchange for the monthly fee of fifteen lire, which the family could not afford to pay, Sister Pia and her mother agreed to take care of the washing and ironing of the laundry of Giovanni Crisostomo and two other Capuchin students. Every Saturday the clean laundry was delivered to the monastery and the laundry that needed to be washed was picked up. Sometimes, when Sister Pia's younger brother was unable to deliver the laundry, she would take his place. On one occasion when Sister Pia knocked on the monastery door, she was greeted by Padre Pio rather than the regular doorkeeper. She was both surprised and elated to see Padre Pio standing right in front of her. After she handed him the laundry, he asked her to wait a moment. He came back with a large bar of chocolate. "This is for you," he said. "I know how much you like chocolate." In the monastery of Our Lady of Grace, Brother Giovanni Crisostomo had been given the job of assisting Padre Pio with many of his daily tasks. Every morning he went to Padre Pio's cell and helped him wash his wounds. He would describe in detail, the terrible wounds on Padre Pio's body. Although the stigmata caused great pain and suffering to Padre Pio, he never complained, and that made Brother Giovanni Crisostomo admire him all the more. Later, Brother Giovanni Crisostomo was sent as a missionary to East Africa where he contracted malaria and passed away at the young age of thirty-two years. Padre Pio was very grieved when he learned about his death. As time passed, Sister Pia D'Apolito felt the call to a religious vocation and after much prayer and reflection, she made application to the Dominican congregation and was accepted. Later, she was sent to the monastery of St. Anthony in Gubbio, Italy, a town that was made famous by St. Francis of Assisi. From time to time she was able to return to San Giovanni Rotondo for a family visit. She spent most of the days in the church at Our Lady of Grace because she wanted to be close to Padre Pio. Throughout her life, he remained her inspiration.

Pray to St. Michael the Archangel

In the early 1950's, my brother, Francis Briguori, made a trip from Naples to San Giovanni Rotondo to see Padre Pio. He was able to make his confession to him. While making his confession, he told Padre Pio that he wanted to join the Navy but did not think he would be accepted because he had a heart defect. Padre Pio looked at him with a very piercing gaze and said, "Tu Vai, Kapish!"which means, "You go, do you understand!" At the end of the confession Padre Pio told my brother to pray to St. Michael the Archangel. He said to my brother, "Michael is your name, too." My brother's name is Francis Mario Michael Briguori. He was so completely taken aback that Padre Pio knew his name that when he left the confessional, he told all the people waiting in the sacristy, "I can't believe it, he knew my name!" Right after that, my brother enlisted in the Navy. On the day that he went in for his medical examination, there were many other young men there who were also having their medical exams. When my brother's name was called, he was told, "Tu Vai" the very same words that Padre Pio had said to him. Evidently he looked so healthy that he was waved on ahead of the others and was accepted without a physical exam. My brother had a wonderful career in the Navy working in the field of shortwave communication. He traveled to many different parts of the world and was never sick nor troubled by any problems with his heart. My brother turned 82 years old this year, 2007. He told me that as long as he lives, he will never be able to forget the way Padre Pio looked at him with those beautiful, piercing eyes. – Enrichetta Spinelli

We'll Get Rid of the Pain Once and For All

Soon after I was released from the hospital, I was in terrible pain like I had never suffered before. I had a dream that I was walking with Padre Pio. I asked him if he could help me get rid of some of the terrible pain I was experiencing. He said, "We'll do exactly that. We'll get rid of it once and for all." I felt extreme relief. All of my pain disappeared and has not returned to this day. I feel great! – Jerry Jones

Someone in Heaven was Praying for Me

I was raised in the Pentecostal church as my father and my relatives on his side were all Pentecostals. My mother was a Catholic. However, she never taught me anything about her faith and then she passed away due to kidney disease. When I was 36 years old my health started declining. A friend gave me a book about Padre Pio and one day when I was at the hospital, while waiting to see the doctor, I started reading the book. I wanted to learn more about my mother's Catholic faith. That day, the doctor told me that I had kidney failure. In 2003, I started on kidney dialysis. I had other serious health problems as well. I had an enlarged heart and on one occasion I went into cardiac arrest. I collapsed and was in a place of total darkness. I felt myself pushing frantically against a black wall. I could hear my two daughters in the next room. All I could think of was to ask God not to let me die. I am a single parent and I wanted to live to see my girls grow up. I survived the experience but it was very frightening. My doctor told me I was very lucky to be alive. My neighbor invited me and my daughters to go to church with her and I began studying the Catholic faith with the parish priest, Father Francis. However, I was getting sicker and sicker each day. I had been on the kidney transplant list for one year. In 2007, I started a novena to Padre Pio, for healing. I would pray the novena while on dialysis. I became friends with a lady named Patsy who was on the dialysis machine next to mine. We talked together about Padre Pio and she too was praying to him. On the ninth day of the novena, while I was on the dialysis machine, I raised a cross I was holding and kissed it and before I could even begin the novena prayer to Padre Pio, I heard one of the nurses shouting for joy and saying to me, "We have a kidney for you!" Patsy was so happy for me that she began to cry. Three days earlier I had told Patsy that I was so tired and in so much pain that I was ready to die. I had the kidney transplant and am doing so much better. Father Francis told me that there was someone in Heaven who was praying for me. I immediately knew that it was Padre Pio and my mother. My daughters and I were baptized into the Catholic church in December. We chose Pia as our confirmation names. – Maria Giuseppa Pia Camilla

He was Indefinable

I made the trip to San Giovanni Rotondo, very curious to see for myself this extraordinary friar who I had seen so many times in newspapers and magazines. When Padre Pio entered the sacristy, I was only just able to see him. He was accompanied by two friars to protect him from the crowd. When he came down for Vespers, I was able to observe him well and from close up. I received such an impression that, still to this day, after having got to know him well from many visits, am unable to describe. He was a figure, dare I say, indefinable. He was fatherly, austere, sullen, happy, sarcastic, ironic. His eyes scrutinized you as if they wanted to penetrate your very flesh and they forced you to lower your eyes... The first thing I experienced when I was in Padre Pio's presence was a marvelous perfume which seemed to me to be the fragrance of violets. After my confession to him, I asked for his blessing for myself and all of my family. He placed his hands on my head and said, "This is also for your family. Young man, always be good." – Alfredo Lapertina

My Prayer is That You Go to Heaven

I had developed heart trouble and along with palpitations, I could often sleep only in a sitting position....During his Mass on the first morning of my visit to San Giovanni Rotondo, I bombarded Padre Pio continuously in thought, asking him to obtain the favor of a healing for me. Toward midday I saw him in the monastery. Addressing me as though I had actually spoken to him, he said in a calm and gentle voice, "Listen to me. My prayer for you is that you go to Heaven. Let that be enough for you. And naturally, do pray for me with the same intention."... Some time later and on several occasions in the course of normal conversation, Padre Pio placed the palm of his right hand and therefore its wound against my heart. Since then, there has been no more heart trouble. – John McCaffrey

I Tried to Help You

My husband, Ricardo and I made a pilgrimage to San Giovanni Rotondo in 2005 to visit the church and friary where Padre Pio spent so many years of his life. It was a beautiful experience. We stayed at a hotel close by and one of the employees there was named Louie. He helped us in many ways, especially by giving us information on how to make a pilgrimage to the shrine of St. Michael the Archangel which is near San Giovanni Rotondo. Padre Pio, in his younger years, had also visited the shrine of St. Michael the Archangel and he often encouraged people to go there. Louie told us that his father had lived in the same area where Padre Pio lived and he had met Padre Pio. One night Louie's father had a vivid dream. In his dream, he saw Padre Pio who said to him, "Get up at once and get your animals because they are being stolen at this very moment." The dream was so vivid that Louie's father woke up, but he did not feel well so he decided not get up to check on his animals. The next morning he discovered that they had been stolen. The next time he went to the church, Padre Pio shook his head and simply said, "I tried to help you." – Dolores Valadez

Confession

I had prayed and asked Padre Pio to help so that my dad would go to confession. He had not gone since he was first married and that was 48 years ago. When I used to ask him to go to confession, he would get very angry. He went to confession on Good Friday of this year. To me this is a miracle. There is no doubt in my mind. Padre Pio continues his work from above and I thank him. – Name Withheld

Mobile

I thank and praise God for having granted my request through the intercession of Padre Pio. After three years in a wheelchair, walker, cane, etc. and being told by doctors that nothing could be done, I am now mobile. I did not pray for a cure. I prayed that I might be healed enough so that I could attend daily Mass. I thank the Lord for working His marvels through His holy servant, Padre Pio. – Mrs. F. R. Woodley

The Next Morning, I Had a Strong Urge to go to Confession

My mother had a friend who was going to have a relic of Padre Pio brought to her home by a priest. She invited my mother to come to her house on the day that the priest was scheduled to visit. The gathering was to be at 1:00 in the afternoon. My mother invited me to go with her but I was not interested. I had never heard of Padre Pio so I declined the invitation. About five minutes before the set time of the gathering, I suddenly changed my mind and decided to go with my mother. When we arrived at her friend's house, there were about six people there. One had cancer and several of the others were sick. The priest passed Padre Pio's glove to each person. The people held the glove and prayed in silence for their needs. At that time, I was not a practicing Catholic. I did not know what to pray for when the glove was passed to me. I felt that my life was going along fine and that I had nothing to ask for so I prayed for my children. While holding the glove, I began to cry. I thought that was indeed strange since I did not know anything about Padre Pio. The next morning when I woke up, I had a strong urge to go to confession. I had not been to confession in twenty years. I made my confession and told the priest about Padre Pio's relic. I told him that after I held Padre Pio's relic, something changed inside of me. The priest told me that I was in a state of grace. I have gone to Mass every Sunday since that day, six years ago when I held Padre Pio's glove in my hand. I do pray to St. Pio and I trust in him as an intercessor with our Lord. – Stephanie Nicolo

The Blessed Little Hand

In 2005, I went on a pilgrimage to San Giovanni Rotondo. While there, we celebrated Mass next to Padre Pio's tomb. After that, I had a great desire to learn more about Padre Pio. When I returned home, I ordered a statue of Padre Pio from a Catholic organization. The statue arrived with one hand missing. I was so disappointed that I started crying. However, I found the little hand wrapped up and in the box. I did not have any strength in my body at the time and I was in alot of pain. I took the little hand of Padre Pio's in my own and prayed. I have been pain free ever since. I thank God and I thank Padre Pio. I have taken the little hand to the hospital on a number of occasions and have prayed with the patients there. The blessed little hand has helped alot of people, including stroke victims and many others. – Socorro Zamora

I Prayed for Padre Pio's Intercession in my Marriage

I am from the Philippines and I work as a Sports Events Specialist. My job requires a lot of traveling abroad. I was on a work assignment in Jakarta, Indonesia when my husband emailed me to say that he wanted a separation. The pain that his words caused me cannot be described. I went to the Catholic Cathedral in Jakarta and spoke to a priest about my marriage situation. The priest told me that I should remain with my husband. Several days later I went back to the Cathedral for Sunday Mass and spoke to another priest. He gave me the same message as the first priest. I prayed for guidance in reading the Holy Scriptures and when I opened my Bible, there were the words of Jesus on divorce. I was calling my husband on the phone and sending him text messages but he would not answer them or communicate with me. I prayed to Padre Pio for the healing of my marriage. One night I had a dream. I dreamed that I had come back from my work abroad and there was an old man in my house. The hood of his black coat was pulled up on his head. In my dream, my husband was there in the house too. He was smiling at me and he embraced me with love. All was well. After that dream, I felt stronger emotionally. I felt I was not alone in facing my problems. I continued to pray to Padre Pio for his intercession. When I finished my job assignment and returned to my home in the Philippines, I was nervous. I did not know what to expect. It turned out to be one of the most beautiful homecomings I ever had. The love that my husband expressed to me was something that I had not felt from him for a long time. I believe that it was Padre Pio in my dream, telling me that he was praying for me. – Malyn – Philippines

Strength in Time of Need

Until recently I was only vaguely aware of Padre Pio. However, I entered the most traumatic period of my life and had very difficult decisions to make and to abide by. Previously, I had similar decisions to make, but always failed miserably and lapsed back into very heartbreaking situations. This time though, I found two magazines of Padre Pio. The articles in these magazines, especially the Padre's writings on suffering, filled me with so much grace, faith in Jesus, and strength, that, thank God and Padre Pio, I have taken the right road and made the right decisions. Each time I face moments of depression, I read Padre Pio's writings, and before long, I fell greatly helped. – Name Withheld

I Was Wounded in Vietnam

On September 23,1968, about 12:00 in the afternoon, I was wounded in Vietnam. I was an Army Field Artillery officer attached to an armored cavalry battalion. As a forward observer, I was responsible for artillery support. We came under enemy fire and I was wounded in the chest by small arms fire.The impact of the bullet knocked me down and the fire fight continued, while my Radio Telephone Operator bandaged my chest and gave me a shot of morphine. He laid me in the bottom of a tracked vehicle as the fighting elevated. It took about 15-30 minutes to get a helicopter evacuation in to take me and the other wounded to the city of Chu Lai where there was a hospital. During this entire time I was conscious although I almost lost consciousness several times. While laying there waiting to be evacuated, my whole brief life of 23 years passed in front of me. I prayed to God to let me live. I was newly married and prayed that He would let me return to my wife. God gave me another chance that day. I don't remember when I was introduced to Padre Pio, but I do know that Padre Pio died on September 23, 1968 and I believe that he died about the same time that God gave me a second chance. I have a special devotion to Padre Pio and daily incorporate his Efficacious Novena to the Sacred Heart of Jesus and his meditation after Holy Communion into my daily prayer life. – Gerry Murphy

Padre Pio Put His Hand on my Head

When I was at school, I used to get dreadful headaches. When I left school, I joined Aer Lingus airlines and was able to make a trip to San Giovanni Rotondo in February 1965. My friend Brenda accompanied me on the trip and we were both able to speak to Padre Pio and to kiss his hand. After he greeted both of us, he started to walk away and had only taken several steps when he stopped and turned toward us once again. He put his hand on Brenda's head and then on mine. I had not said a word to Padre Pio about my headaches but after he touched me, that was the end of the headaches. – Nuala Wall

A True Spiritual Father

Elidé Bellomo was one of Padre Pio's earliest spiritual daughters. She first came to San Giovanni Rotondo in 1946. Padre Pio asked her to stay and help with the many duties of his growing ministry. She helped establish the prayer groups and assisted at his hospital. Elidé was very close to her mother and when her mother died suddenly from a heart attack, Elidé was grief-stricken. She immediately went to Padre Pio.

"Padre," she sobbed, "What am I to do now?" Listen to me," Padre Pio said. "I am now your entire family; mother, father, brother, anything you want. Your mother is in Heaven. Let us concentrate on trying to get there ourselves.We must do our best to deserve it." Elidé found great comfort in his words.

A Medical Miracle

My family and extended family are from Italy and some of them knew Padre Pio. My grandfather, Cosmo Orlando, who was a farmer, remembered Padre Pio from the early days. He said that Padre Pio was always the one boy who acted as mediator when disputes rose among friends. My father was twelve years old when he moved to America. His mother took him to the monastery to say goodbye to Padre Pio. My father remembers vividly taking hold of Padre Pio's hand when saying goodbye to him. In 1958, while on deck in a baseball contest, I was struck in the head with the bat from the player who had just struck out at the plate. I was eight years old at the time. I suffered a double skull fracture and underwent an eight-hour operation. My life was in the hands of two wonderful neurosurgeons, Dr. Greenberg and Dr. Fromm. Although, I survived the operation, Dr.Greenberg informed my mother that the prognosis was very dim. I probably would suffer permanent brain damage and thus a normal life was not likely. My grandfather, who had an undying belief in Padre Pio, possessed one of his gloves. It was placed on my forehead in the hospital. When I was released from the hospital, I continued my recuperation and a month later I was able to return to school. After that, I never looked back, even though a plate was inserted in my head the following year. I remained under Dr. Greenberg's care until I turned twenty-one years old. He always told my mother and myself that he could not explain my recovery, especially since a part of my brain had to be removed from the left lobe. Dr. Greenberg used to say that someone else or something else assisted me. He concluded that my recovery was a medical miracle. My father retains the glove of Padre Pio to this day. – Joseph Orlando

Peace of Mind

I have been praying to Padre Pio for a few years now. Since praying to him I have stopped taking tranquilizers and am free of panic attacks. But most importantly, I now have a strong faith and I believe my faith will see me through anything. Everything in my life has changed for the better with the help of Padre Pio, our Lord and our Lady. – Name Withheld

I Ask for Your Prayers

I ask for your prayers as I am at a place in my life where I am in great need of God's help and direction. Some time ago, I had a very vivid dream whereby I saw a man with a dark robe on and a beard. In my dream, the man said to me, "I was wondering if you would like to become a nun, after your children are raised?" I told him that I did not think so. But I said that I did have some things that I wanted to do for God once my children were raised. He said to me, "But what are you planning to do for God right now?" Shortly after that dream, I went to confession to Father Solcia at Our Lady of the Rosary. At the end of the confession, Father Solcia handed me a prayer card and said, "Padre Pio is praying for you." On the prayer card was a picture of the same man I had seen in my dream. Below the picture were the words, "Padre Pio." – Name Withheld

I Asked Padre Pio to Send My Husband a Sign

I have been blessed by praying Padre Pio's prayers, especially the Novena to the Sacred Heart of Jesus. I prayed to Padre Pio and asked him to save my marriage for I am currently in the process of a divorce. On June 13, 2008 we went to court regarding the divorce. I prayed to Padre Pio with great devotion for his intercession. Four days later, my husband told me that he no longer hated me and that he wanted to talk to me about our situation. I prayed to Padre Pio to guide my husband and send him a sign regarding what he should do with his life. My husband told me that he had a dream in which he and I and our son were all together. Glory be to God! I know that Padre Pio has heard me and prayed for me to the Lord. – Name Withheld

Carrying Me

I have a great devotion to Padre Pio. It began in 2002 when I visited Italy. In the past six years, my family has had many problems. My grand daughter was diagnosed with a rare blood cancer. My daughter was also diagnosed with cancer. My stepdaughter had a hole in her heart and was in very serious condition. Also, my son suffered a heart attack. To each one of them I gave either a Padre Pio medal or a Padre Pio statue and told them to pray to Padre Pio and ask for his help. I thank God and Padre Pio that they are all doing well now. In January 2008, I was diagnosed with lung cancer. I am seventy-eight years old and have other serious health problems. I have a pacemaker and defibulator and also a bad heart. I needed surgery but my doctor was not optimistic about my chances of surviving an operation. I gave my doctor a medal of Padre Pio and told him that I had complete confidence that Padre Pio would see me through. I was operated on at Sloan-Kettering Hospital in New York City and my left lung was removed. I developed an infection after the surgery and spent three months in the hospital. After that I was transferred to Burke Rehabilitation Hospital in White Plains, New York. One day, one of the nurses' aides came in my room and told me that she had a dream about me. "I have never had a dream about one of my patients before," she said. I asked her about the dream. She looked at the Padre Pio statue that I had in my room and pointed at it. "I dreamed that he was carrying you," she said. I am recovering slowly from the surgery. I continue my devotion to Padre Pio and the Blessed Mother and urge everyone to pray the Rosary daily. – John Giumarra

Padre Pio Touched Me and the Pain was Gone

In the early fall of 2007, I sprained my foot. The pain increased throughout the day and by the evening, the pain was so great that I could not walk at all. That night I had to be carried to my bed. I was worried and I was wondering how I would manage since I could not walk. I finally fell asleep. That night I dreamed that I was in a large church and I was laying on the floor because I was unable to walk. Padre Pio was led into the church by two men. He knelt down near me to pray. There was a relic of St. Anthony in the church and that was why he had come. Before he left, he put his hand out and touched my foot where the sprain had occurred. Then he touched my hand. After that, many other people began to reach out to him. I woke up immediately from the dream and noticed that my foot was no longer throbbing. In fact, I was able to get up and walk to the other end of the house by myself. The injury healed quite quickly and there was no permanent damage. – Krysten Hager

My Friend Brought Padre Pio's Prayers to us at the Hospital

My brother, Mateo Garcia, was hospitalized at the Chong Hua General Hospital in the Philippines on August 20, 2007. He suffered from bleeding peptic ulcer disease, chronic liver disease, sepsis, osteomyletis, cellulitis and intravascular disease. He also had internal bleeding that the doctors could not alleviate. He was given more than 70 blood transfusions. I asked the doctor to tell us the real score about my brother's condition so that we could prepare ourselves. The doctor told us that it was just a matter of time. Mateo was going to die. My brother Ricardo and I went to Mateo's bedside in the Intensive Care Unit and we all prayed together. We recited the prayers our parents taught us when we were little – "Jesus, Mary and Joseph, I give you my heart and my soul; Jesus, Mary and Joseph, assist me in my last agony; Jesus, Mary and Joseph I breathe forth my soul in peace with you." When Mateo fell asleep, Ricardo and I left the hospital, feeling very forlorn. We begged God to give us the strength to accept His will for our brother. The next day, one of the Chinese doctors gave my brother a herbal medicine. A good friend stopped by the hospital and brought us a framed picture of Padre Pio, Padre Pio's Novena to the Sacred Heart of Jesus and a prayer leaflet with a tiny relic of Padre Pio on it. Mateo and I kissed the relic and returned it to my friend. Earnestly and from our hearts, Ricardo and I prayed the prayers of Padre Pio with Mateo. The following day, when we came to see Mateo in the ICU, we learned that the bleeding had stopped altogether. My brother was discharged from the hospital on the 15th of September. He is now recuperating at home. Thanks be to God and to the intercession of St. Pio! – Josefina Garcia Serranilla

Padre Pio Started Laughing

I saw Padre Pio in person when I was growing up. It was in 1951 and I was 10 years old at the time. My mother and I attended his Mass. I was very impressed by him. His tiny church could barely hold a handful of peasants. The Mass was very, very early in the morning and outside it was freezing. The church however was very warm inside. It was a great experience. My mother made her confession to Padre Pio. At one point during the confession, he started laughing and he said to my mother, "If these things you are confessing were sins, then we would all be in paradise." She received absolution from Padre Pio. – Vittorio Manunta

Padre Pio said, "There will be Victory"

I was born near Bagdad, Iraq and baptized in the parish of the Virgin Mary of the Holy Heart. When I was still a baby, my parents decided to move the family to the United States to escape the dangers of the country and so that my brothers and sisters and I might have a better life. It was a great sacrifice for them to leave their country and all that was dear to them but they knew it was for the best. I learned about Padre Pio in 2006 and started attending the Padre Pio prayer group in San Diego. On occasion, I brought my mother with me and she liked it very much. 2007 was a devastating year for the Chaldean Catholic community in Badgad. My mother became very distraught over the tragedies that were occurring there. Chaldean Catholic bishops, priests, and deacons were being threatened daily. Extremist terrorist groups warned them that they would be killed if they continued to have Mass in their churches. My mother watched the news on television one day and saw several of the Catholic churches in Baghdad that were destroyed by roadside bombings. She was filled with anxiety and wept over the tragic events. She had a great love for the parish she had attended when she lived in Iraq and feared that it would also be leveled just like the others. One evening when my mother was very sad, I took her to the Padre Pio prayer group with me. When we came home, I placed a picture of Padre Pio next to my parents' bed. That night she had a vivid dream. In her dream, she was praying and pleading that God would protect her parish in Baghdad. Padre Pio suddenly appeared in her dream. He raised his hands and she could see the marks of the stigmata. He said to her in Aramaic, "Do not worry. There will be victory." When my mother woke up, she was filled with a great sense of peace. My parents' parish in Baghdad is still standing today. Although one window was shattered and an outer wall was damaged by an act of violence, the church was repaired and Mass is said there regularly. My parents have remained very devoted to Padre Pio. –Zina Hallak

I Prayed to Padre Pio to Help Me

Recently I was falsely accused in a custody battle and put through a living hell. All the time, I prayed to Padre Pio to help me and I carried a relic of his with me at all times. I received his intercession for my name has been cleared. The person who was responsible for the false accusations was held on six charges of contempt of court. – Name Withheld

My Grandfather Encouraged me to Pray

My grandfather, George Bartoli, went to see Padre Pio twice in his life, the first time in 1957. He was able to make his confession to Padre Pio. Usually confessions to Padre Pio lasted just a few minutes, but after the confession was over, Padre Pio and my grandfather talked for a long time. It seemed as though Padre Pio was very happy to speak with him and was in no hurry to end the conversation. My grandfather was from the northern part of Italy. He and Padre Pio talked about many things, including the wine and good food from the northern region of Italy. My grandfather had a handkerchief with him of a friend who was dying of cancer. He spoke to Padre Pio about her. "She will be in Paradise soon," Padre Pio said. Then he blessed the handkerchief saying that perhaps it would comfort her. My grandfather had always been a worrier. "Stay calm," Padre Pio repeated to him over and over. My grandfather said that Padre Pio had very piercing, dark eyes. It was through my grandfather's love for Padre Pio that I came to know and love him as well. I had drifted away from my Catholic faith and had become involved in the New Age movement. My husband and I separated and then divorced. I was living alone with my daughter and I was depressed. My grandfather was praying very hard for me to return to my faith. I began to have double vision and then blurry vision and finally no vision at all. I was ready to get a seeing-eye dog. The doctor thought that I had a stroke but later I was diagnosed with Myasthenia Gravis, a neuromuscular disease. The muscles in my eyelids became so weak that I could not even hold them open. I was set to have an operation on my eyes but there was no guarantee that my sight would be restored. My grandfather drove me to a final doctor appointment before the surgery. He gave me a relic of Padre Pio and told me to pray to him. I went into the examination room and before the doctor came in, I held the relic over my eyes and prayed and begged Padre Pio to heal me. My grandfather was in the waiting room, praying for me. The doctor examined my eyes and then left the room. He came back and examined them one more time and then left the room again. He came in a third time with another doctor who also examined my eyes. Then they both left. I was quite scared. The doctor came in once again and told me that he wanted to cancel my surgery because he believed that I did not need the operation. The surgery was cancelled. I began to get my vision back and it improved daily. The biggest miracle of all was that because of the healing of my eyes, my faith was restored and also my marriage. My husband and I reconciled and were reunited after being apart for over five years. – Claudia Bartoli-McKinney

I Prayed to St. Pio and Asked Him to Help My Friend

Recently I was praying in the side chapel in our local Cathedral of St. Monica's here in Cairns, North Queensland, Australia. I was praying for a friend of mine who is an atheist and an alcoholic. She also has several diagnosed mental health problems including bipolar disorder and anxiety disorder. I prayed to St. Pio and asked him to help her. There was only one other man in the chapel at the time and as he was leaving, I noticed that he paused to touch the statue of Our Lady. At the moment he touched the statue, I perceived the sweetest fragrance of flowers. I believed it must have come from the man but after he left the chapel, the fragrance remained. I trusted then that St. Pio had heard my prayer. Shortly afterward, I received a message from my friend. She said that quite suddenly she had come to the conclusion that she must do something positive with her life. She has since applied for a good job and with Our Lord's help and mercy and St. Pio's intercession, I believe she is now on a new and positive path. – Name Withheld

The Doctors were Amazed

My mother, Margaret McVeigh, went into a coma and we were told by her doctors that she would not live. We began to pray to Padre Pio and we asked him to give our mother two more years of life. The doctor told us that it would not matter how many prayers we prayed because our mother was going to die. He believed that she would die within two days. Much to the doctors amazement and also to our own, our mother came out of the coma. She lived for two more years, the years that we asked Padre Pio for. We thank him from the bottom of our hearts. – Elizabeth and Bernadette McVeigh

Padre Pio's Hand was So Warm

I live in Belfast, Ireland and one cold and windy winter morning, I went to pray in the chapel at the parish of St. Agnes. It was raining heavily that day. Outside it felt colder than the coldness of my heart and home. The night before had been a bitter night with family problems and I was broken-hearted. I entered the chapel of St. Agnes and kept the hood of my coat up hoping that no one would notice my tears. When I finished my prayers, I left the chapel by the side door. I was amazed to see a life-size bronze statue of Padre Pio at the foot of the grotto of Our Lady of Lourdes. I had never noticed it before as St. Agnes is not my regular parish. Still crying, I went over and put my hand in Padre Pio's and begged for his help. Because it was such a cold day, I was taken aback by the warmth of the statue's hand. I wondered how it was possible that it could feel so warm. A few days later I returned to pray but also to see if the hand was still warm. The hand was stone cold. Over the last few years, I have visited the grotto a number of times and have touched the statue's hand. It has been cold ever since. It is my belief that Padre Pio personally comforted me on that Saturday morning. My mind was in such turmoil and my heart was so cold that he gave me some of his warmth. I love Padre Pio and I know he has helped me in many ways over the years. – Name Withheld

A Heavenly Light

In May 1981, our thirteen-month-old-son Darren, became very ill with a high fever. My wife and I rushed him to St. Joseph's Hospital in Clonmel (County Limerick, Ireland). He was diagnosed with bacterial meningitis. By the time we got him to the hospital, he was semi-conscious. The doctors were unable to set up an i.v. for him because his veins had collapsed. A friend of ours gave us a relic of Padre Pio and a Padre Pio prayer card. We said the prayer many times a day at Darren's bedside. One day I was sitting beside his bed saying the novena prayer to Padre Pio. All of a sudden, my head was lifted toward the ceiling by a strange force under my chin. I saw what appeared to be a little blue light, no bigger than a flashlight bulb. My eyes were dazzled by this little light. It came down from the ceiling very slowly, to the novena prayer in my hand. It shot like a ball of light from the prayer card into Darren's back. I told my wife, Barbara, what I had seen but before she could ask me anything about it, Darren was moving and he opened his eyes. For the first time in a week he called out to us, "mama, daddy." He was released from the hospital one week later. Thanks be to God and to Padre Pio. – James Doyle

The Doctor had a Great Belief in Padre Pio

Padre Pio sought the help of his close friends and collaborators and worked for many years in order to achieve his dream of establishing a fully-equipped, modern-day hospital in San Giovanni Rotondo. He named it the "Home for the Relief of Suffering." On the day of the inauguration, May 5, 1956, Padre Pio offered Mass on the front steps of the hospital while a crowd of 15,000 people looked on. Many people wanted to help Padre Pio in his great work as evidenced by the following story regarding Donato Di Ge: Donato Di Ge visited San Giovanni Rotondo on January 20, 1960. It was a Sunday and he was spurred on by the usual irresistible desire to be near Padre Pio for a few days. In the sacristy of the church, he noticed for the first time, posters everywhere, asking for blood donors for the Home for the Relief of Suffering. Those who were sick in Padre Pio's hospital were in need of blood transfusions. Donato wanted with all his heart to answer the call of the hospital. His desire to donate blood was so great that his first impulse was to go to the Home for the Relief of Suffering at once. But then he remembered how he had recently had an operation for a perforated ulcer and had nearly died. He also had other health problems including very low blood pressure as well as chronic pain in his gall bladder. He decided that it would be best to consult Padre Pio about the matter. Toward the middle of the morning, shortly after Mass, Donato was able to speak to Padre Pio briefly. Donato told Padre Pio about his various health issues and then asked him if it would be all right for him to be a blood donor for the hospital. Padre Pio looked at him with a penetrating gaze and then said to him kindly, "Well, what are you waiting for?" Donato went straight over to the hospital where the doctor in charge gave him a physical examination. When the doctor took his blood pressure and saw how low it was, he explained the hospital's policy to Donato. "I am very sorry," the doctor said. "Because you have an abnormal blood pressure reading, you will not be allowed to be a donor." "Doctor," Donato replied, "I spoke to Padre Pio about this a few moments ago and he wanted me to come over here to see you." The doctor had great faith in Padre Pio. If Padre Pio had encouraged Donato to donate his blood, it was good enough for the doctor. He told Donato that he would give his approval. As Donato continued to donate blood to Padre Pio's hospital, his blood pressure showed a marked improvement and the chronic pain that had plagued him for such a long time began to diminish. In other words, the more blood he gave, the better his health became. He was able to make fifty-two blood donations to the Home for the Relief of Suffering.

"Come and Find Me," Padre Pio said

I was praying to the Infant Jesus, the Sacred Heart and the Holy Spirit for my brother-in-law, when one night I dreamed of Padre Pio. He said, "Come and find me." I woke up and remembered that I had the novena prayer to Padre Pio and the Sacred Heart somewhere in the house. I immediately went looking for it. I found it without any trouble. I then started the novena to Padre Pio and the Sacred Heart. My prayers have been answered. – Linda Della Badia

Padre Pio's Words went Straight to my Heart

About three and a half years ago, I was in a troubled situation with my boyfriend and was very hurt by some of his actions. During this period of agony, I prayed and begged Jesus and Mother Mary to help me. I also prayed daily to St. Benedict, St. Joseph, St. Therese of the Child Jesus and St. Anthony. One day I walked into St. Peter and Paul church in Singapore and at the entrance to the church I saw these words on the bulletin board, "Pray, hope, and don't worry." The words lingered in my mind and kept surfacing. Deep in my heart I sensed that they were a message for me. Some days later I returned to the church because I wanted to see those words once again. I looked on the bulletin board but they were no longer there. Recently, I was at St. Therese church bookstore and noticed a single copy of a book about Padre Pio titled, "Pray, Hope, and Don't Worry." I knew instantly that I wanted to buy it. At that time, all that I knew about Padre Pio was that he was a priest and that he had the stigmata. Not long after I purchased the book, I found out that my name was on the work force reduction list at the company where I work. I was going to be laid off from my job. The shock was so great that I felt that I could not accept the news. For some reason, I picked up "Pray, Hope, and Don't Worry" and began to read it. Reading the testimonies in the book had a transforming effect on me and gave me a new understanding of my Catholic faith, reverence for the Eucharist, and a deep faith in Jesus and love for Mother Mary. I did not find my way to Padre Pio, but Padre Pio found his way to me, in order to save me, to change me, and to bless me. Through these two major events in my life which caused me deep sorrow, the issues with my boyfriend and the loss of my job, Padre Pio came as a friend to encourage me and strengthen my faith. I treasure his words, his strict code of conduct, his wisdom, his humility, and his great love for God's people. Thank you Padre Pio, for your love. – Vivian Chew

"Everything Depends on God," Padre Pio said

My mother Angela had always been very devoted to Padre Pio and also to the Madonna Paradiso (the Madonna of Paradise) the patroness of the town where she grew up in Sicily. When my brother Joseph was diagnosed with cancer, my mother prayed constantly to Padre Pio and to the Madonna, asking for a miracle. But a cure was not to be. My brother died in 2009 after suffering for one and a half years. My mother became so distraught and so heartbroken at my brother's death that she told the family she no longer believed in God or in the power of the saints. She said that she was going to take all the statues, sacred paintings, and religious articles out of her house and that she would never pray again. She was finished with religion forever. Several weeks later, my mother told me that something amazing had happened. In the middle of the night she saw Padre Pio who said to her, "I prayed as hard as I could for your son, but it was not meant to be. As he raised his hand and pointed upward he said, "Everything depends on God." The experience was so vivid that it woke my mother up from a sound sleep. She began to wonder, "Was it a dream or did Padre Pio actually pay me a visit?" She finally got back to sleep only to have the very same dream, exact in all the details. She again awakened and this time she stayed up for the rest of the night. The dream brought closure and peace to my mother. She never again spoke against the Church. She took up her practice of prayer and her devotions, just as she had in the past and remained faithful until her death. – Margaret Gigante

At Padre Pio's Tomb

On June 23, 1985 I had a very serious motorcycle accident causing severe and traumatic injuries to my left leg and hip. Fortunately, the doctors were able to save the leg, but I was left with pain, and after walking any distance I resorted to the use of a cane. In June 1994, my wife and I had the good fortune to visit Our Lady of Grace church in San Giovanni Rotondo and the tomb of Padre Pio. The instant that I walked into the church, I felt a strange warm sensation in my left leg. The feeling grew in intensity and as I neared the tomb of Padre Pio, I started to cry. I then explained to my wife what I had experienced. We both thanked God and knew that Padre Pio had somehow interceded for me. We made the Stations of the Cross on the grounds outside the church and I felt no pain in my leg nor needed any assistance. Today, I no longer require the use of a cane and there is no longer any pain at all in my leg. – Francis Cotter

It is a Beautiful Prayer," the Young Man Told Me

I work as a volunteer chaplain at a nearby hospital. Recently, when I went to the hospital there was a note for me that one of the patients requested a visit. I went to the room and found a very nice looking young man in his late twenties. He told me that he was in a lot of pain and also that he was very depressed because he had a relapse and had started using drugs again. He was in the hospital for drug related problems. He was so happy that I had come to visit him. He told me that his father had introduced him to hard drugs when he was just thirteen years old and they used drugs together on a regular basis. He said that due to drugs, four times he had gone into cardiac arrest and had been declared clinically dead. He had a stroke on one occasion due to his drug abuse and was paralyzed and unable to speak for a time. Fortunately his speech and movement both had returned. However, he had started using drugs again and was very disappointed in himself. I told him that even though he had "fallen off the wagon," so to speak, God still loved him and he should never stop trying to be free of his addiction. All the time we were talking, the nurses and therapists were coming into his room making it difficult for us to talk. "This is just my luck," he said to me. "I finally get a visitor, and the nurses won't give us a chance to talk." I handed him the prayer of Padre Pio, "Stay with me, Lord," and told him I would come back later in the afternoon. When I returned that afternoon, the young man looked so much happier. He said he loved the prayer of Padre Pio so much that he had called his mother on the telephone and read it to her. The prayer touched him so much that he cried while reading it to his mother. He told her that he was thinking that he should go back to the Catholic Church. He had been away from the Church for a long time. His mother told him that she too, would think about returning. After the phone call, he fell asleep and he said that he had not slept so peacefully and so deeply in a long time. I know that Padre Pio's prayers are powerful and transforming. I have seen it on many occasions. I thank God for the blessing of seeing that power working in that young man's heart that day. – Deacon Ron Allen

I Prayed for my Sister

My sister was facing a very hard time financially and her salary could not meet even a quarter of her needs, which included caring for four children. She took on a second job to try to meet her bills. This meant that she had to work about fourteen hours a day. I decided to start a novena to Padre Pio asking him to help her. The headmistress of a large boarding primary school spoke to me and told me she was going to offer my sister a job. The salary that was offered was twice what my sister was making before. There were also many other benefits that were offered to her. I was surprised at the immediacy with which Padre Pio obtained this favor for my sister. – M.N.K.

My Mother Told me How Lucky I Was

I had lived in England for many years and to be honest, I did not live a good or holy life. I began seeing a man and I became pregnant. From that point on, the man no longer wanted anything to do with me. I moved back to Ireland to live with my parents as they said they would help support me and my baby. It was a very dark and painful time in my life. My son was born in November, 2006. It was a long and difficult labor and there were some serious complications. A few days after the birth of my son, I became quite ill, both physically and emotionally. The wound in my abdomen from the caeserean section deliver had opened and was bleeding. My mother brought a medal of Padre Pio to the hospital and told me to put it under my pillow. I thought that my mother was very silly to suggest such a thing. I had never heard of Padre Pio before and I had no interest in learning about him either. I assumed he was a biblical figure and it annoyed me that my mother believed that Padre Pio could save me. I thought no more about the matter. I was finally discharged from the hospital but my wound was still open and bleeding after ten days. My parents took care of my son so that I could sleep at night. One night I had a dream in which I was a little girl again, maybe seven or eight years old. I was standing in a field. I could see trees at the top of a hill. They were not like any of the trees I have ever seen in either England or Ireland but seemed to be from a foreign country. They looked like orange trees. Underneath the trees was a man dressed in a long brown cloak. He had a beard. I felt full of happiness just to be with him. He placed his hand on my head and then he hugged me. In my dream, I saw myself with a big smile on my face. When I woke up, I did not think too much about the dream but as I was changing the dressing on my wound, I discovered that it had healed. It was not even bleeding. It was still painful but all the signs of the open wound had disappeared. I felt like a new person. I did not tell my mother about the dream, but when I showed her how the wound had healed, she could not believe it. Later, I came across a book on Padre Pio and saw a picture of him on the cover. Sure enough, he was the man I saw in my dream. I then told my mother. My eyes still fill with tears whenever I think about it. My mother told me how lucky I was that Padre Pio chose to help me. – C. Tobin

Padre Pio Said to my Mother, You Are Healed

I was raised in the Catholic Church but after a time, I lapsed. I lost interest in seeking God. I was not an atheist, for I never denied God's existence, but I lacked faith. By profession, I am a medical doctor and also a scientist. I used to say that I was a Catholic but I did not experience an authentic spiritual life until recently, when my mother, Telma Ferrari became ill. In 2008, my mother, was diagnosed with an inoperable brain tumor. After I received news of the diagnosis, I began to pray two novenas each day for my mother – a novena to Padre Pio and a novena to Our Lady of the Rosary. It was the first time in my life that I had ever prayed a novena. I chose to pray to Padre Pio because I had heard a testimonial of someone who had received a grace through his intercession and I was impressed by the story. After a time, my mother and father joined me in praying the two novenas each day. My mother received chemotherapy and radiation at the MD Anderson Cancer Center in Houston, Texas. During the radiation treatment, she perceived the strong fragrance of roses. It accompanied her for over a month. She had an incredible response to the treatment and all traces of the tumor vanished. On one occasion, when I visited my parents at their home, we watched a movie about the life of Padre Pio. During the movie, a strong and exquisite fragrance of violets suddenly came from my mother's Rosary. I had never experienced anything like that in my life. At that moment, we all had a sense of inner peace. This year, my mother developed cancer of the bone and although we did not lose our faith, we were very concerned. We prayed once again for the intercession of Padre Pio. After the first round of treatments, my mother heard a voice in her home. It was the voice of Padre Pio. He spoke to her in Italian and said, "You are healed." My mother understood the words easily for she speaks both English and Italian. After that, the bone pain that she was experiencing in her lower back went away. She was then able to walk by herself again without using her walker. We went to San Giovanni Rotondo in June of this year, 2010, to express our gratitude for the graces that my mother (and all of us) received from Christ and Our Blessed Mother through the intercession of Padre Pio. I attended Mass with my parents at the church of Santa Maria delle Grazie and I felt moved to tears while I was at this church. They were not tears of sorrow but of joy and peace. While my mother was in the church, she noticed an intense fragrance of violets that lasted about 20 minutes. She felt a great peace in her heart. My mother's second tumor is now in remission. We are planning to visit San Giovanni Rotondo again this year, December 2010 in order to give thanks. – Dr. Fernando Scaglia

Padre Pio said, "Go and Thank our Lord who has Given You a Handsome Grandson."

Dr. Luigi Pancaro was Padre Pio's physician and he worked at the hospital, the Home for the Relief of Suffering, in San Giovanni Rotondo.

In 1954, my husband, Dr. Luigi Pancaro, was urgently summoned by a midwife from San Giovanni Rotondo as she had a very difficult case on her hands which needed a doctor's intervention. In a hurry, he gathered his obstretric instruments and rushed to the home in his little Fiat. It was about a mile from the hospital. The midwife, along with various other women of the neighborhood, had been with the patient for many hours. My husband took charge and everything went well and soon a healthy baby boy was born.

After giving instructions to the midwife about the care of the patient and the child, my husband left to return to the hospital. While driving up the somewhat steep hill, my husband noticed an elderly man coming from the opposite direction. Luigi recognized him as the grandfather of the patient. He slowed down to give the old man the good news but did not have the chance to do so. The grandfather approached him and said, "I know, Dr. Pancaro. Thank you so much. I have a grandson."

Surprised, my husband stopped the car and asked him how he knew. He replied, "Padre Pio told me. While I was praying outside his cell door, Padre Pio said to me, "Go and thank our Lord who has given you a handsome grandson." The puzzling question arose. How did Padre Pio know it was a boy? There were no telephone communications, and above all, the time factor did not permit anyone to reach the old grandfather with the news. Yet Padre Pio knew all about it. – Lina Pancaro

They Drove Back to the Monastery to Thank Padre Pio

My uncle, Eugene (Gene) Grimes, told me of a miracle that occurred through his contact with Padre Pio. Uncle Gene enlisted in the Army Air Corp during World War II and was stationed at the Air Base in Foggia, Italy assigned to the 347 Bombardment Squadron. As a sargeant, he worked on the ground crew as a munitions inspector. Uncle Gene had been a devout Catholic all of his life, and he used to attend Padre Pio's Mass in San Giovanni Rotondo which was not a great distance from the air base. He and the other G.I.'s would take a two and a half-ton truck, called a deuce and a half, up the steep road that led to Padre Pio's monastery. He described Padre Pio as a very humble priest and he was awed by his stigmata. He felt blessed whenever he was in his presence. Uncle Gene had the honor of being an altar server at Padre Pio's Mass. He knew what a great privilege it was. One day after Mass, Padre Pio said to my uncle, "Gino, I want you to be very careful when you go back down the mountain today." He warned him about the brakes on the truck. Uncle Gene assured Padre Pio that he and the other soldiers would all be fine. Before they left, Padre Pio gave them a blessing. On the way down the mountain, the truck lost its brakes and began to pick up speed. The driver fought to keep it on the road. Uncle Gene was sitting in the front passenger's side of the truck. As they came around a blind curve on the narrow and winding road, they saw a massive five ton wrecker directly in front of them. It was about to hit them head-on. Suddenly Uncle Gene's whole life flashed before his eyes, and he believed that he was going to die. Their truck then started to go off the side of the mountain. In an instant, their truck was back on the road but going in the opposite direction, now headed up the mountain. There was no accident, no head-on collision. Uncle Gene and the other soldiers were awed by what had happened and knew that it was a miracle. They returned to the monastery to thank Padre Pio for saving them. They decided not to tell anyone because they were convinced that no one would believe them. In 1945, Uncle Gene received an honorable discharge from the Army and returned to the U.S. and made his home in Worcester, Massachusetts. His was very active in the parish of St. Peter located in Worcester. At that time, very few people in the U.S. had heard of Padre Pio. Uncle Gene remained very devoted to Padre Pio for the rest of his life. – Charles T. Grimes

My Father Returned to Mass after an Absence of 30 Years

My father, Sylvester Gentile had a brilliant mind and worked in the field of electrical engineering. He was a published author and the book that he wrote was a best-seller in the world of engineering and was translated into several languages. He was a good man and he was very kind but he was not religious. He felt that religion was something for women who needed emotional comfort. Personally, he had no use for religion. After my mother died at the young age of 52 years, my father fell into a depression. I gave him two books on Padre Pio which he read with interest. My father knew that Padre Pio's stigmata as well as the miracles that surrounded his life, were scientifically inexplicable. That fact convinced him of the existence of God. The graces that my father received after reading the books on Padre Pio caused him to return to Mass after an absence of 30 years. He began to attend Mass regularly at St. Dorothea's parish in Eatontown, New Jersey. My father then joined the Catholic prayer group that I belonged to. On one occasion, he gave a full presentation at our prayer group on Padre Pio, sharing many stories about his life as well as the scientific studies of his stigmata. It makes sense that God would use science to attract my father and bring him back to the faith! – Pat Hulick

My Teacher Did Not Understand

My daughter and I made a trip to San Giovanni Rotondo and were able to attend Padre Pio's Mass. His face was the most beautiful I have ever seen. It seemed transparent and the color of his skin was exquisite beyond words. My daughter saw a golden light surrounding his form. Upon returning home, and back to my class in sculpture, I immediately began a carving of Padre Pio. My teacher really did not understand my inspiration, and often during the weeks of work on it, showed some disappointment in my choice of subject. One day as my teacher approached me, the strong scent of incense filled the air all about the area I was working in. As we looked about the large studio to find the source of the incense, we discovered that it was coming from my carving of Padre Pio. My teacher then said, "But this is a miracle!" It truly was. His attitude changed immediately and he then helped guide my work until it was completed. – Anna Pardini

Padre Pio was in Contact with God

In 1952, I was a seminarian in the diocese of Pittsburgh and along with another seminarian, Tom Kirby, we went together for our summer vacation to visit some of my relatives in Italy and to see some of the places of pilgrimage in Rome. We had heard of Padre Pio and wanted to visit him so we took a bus from Rome. We were lucky to find lodging in San Giovanni Rotondo with an elderly woman. I can still remember that she cooked macaroni every night (which I wasn't too fond of) for the houseguests. I remember the cold stone floors in her home and the army cots that all the guests slept on. The accommodations were not the most comfortable and as a young seminarian, I felt that we were really roughing it. At the monastery, we got in line to go to Padre Pio for confession and before he entered the confessional we noticed that a woman was bothering him. She kept following him around, insisting that he give her a blessing. She would not leave him alone and he became so annoyed with the woman that he finally lost his patience and said to her in a very stern voice, "You can go to any priest for a blessing. You do not have to come to me. You must leave me alone." Seeing this incident caused Tom and I to lose our courage regarding making our confession to Padre Pio. We decided to leave the confessional line. I knew that Padre Pio had the gift of reading hearts. I did not mind what he might tell me about my future but the idea that he could look into my soul seemed frightening to me. I have always regretted that I did not avail myself of the opportunity to make my confession to him. The Mass was held in an outdoor arcade, right beside the church. I assumed that the reason it was held outdoors was in order to accommodate all of the people who were there. Tom and I were in the very front row, just a few feet from Padre Pio. The sleeves of his vestments were very long, but when he raised his hands during the Mass, I could see the wounds of Christ in his hands very clearly. The reverence with which he celebrated Mass was beautiful. He concentrated on the prayers of the Mass with great intensity and he said the Mass slowly. He seemed to be "somewhere else." I felt that he was in Heaven. He was in contact with God, we were certain of that. I knew in my heart that he was a saint. Father Tom Kirby and I were ordained in the diocese of Pittsburgh in on May 25, 1957, a special day because May 25 is Padre Pio's birthday. This year, 2007, I celebrated 50 years in the priesthood. I never got the chance to return to San Giovanni Rotondo but I would go back in a heartbeat. It was such a beautiful experience. – Father Ernest Paone

Padre Pio was Welcoming Him

I had the honor of knowing a very wonderful man named Fred D'Angelo. Fred went to Mass everyday and he did this throughout his entire life. He lived in Lawrence, Massachusetts and I met him at my parish, "Our Lady of Mt. Carmel." Fred lived in Italy in the 1940's and he used to visit Padre Pio's monastery. He served at the altar at Padre Pio's Mass. He told me that one time he took a pair of Padre Pio's gloves because he wanted to have a souvenir to remember him by. When Padre Pio was looking for his gloves one day, Fred admitted to him that he had taken them. Padre Pio told him that all he had to do was ask, and he would have given them to him. He told Fred never again to take anything that did not belong to him. Then he told him that he was forgiven. Fred also told me that Padre Pio was very annoyed by the crowds of people who constantly pressed in on him, trying to touch his habit, etc. Fred always had a special glow about him whenever he talked to me about Padre Pio. Before Fred passed away, he had to go to a nursing home. He spent all of his time there in prayer and in the chapel saying his Rosary. He told me that Padre Pio had come to him in the hospital. Padre Pio was in a very large place, like a town. It was a pleasant place and everyone was friendly and welcoming. Padre Pio wanted Fred to join him there and was welcoming him. Shortly after that, Fred passed away. – Kay Bonanno

Looking at Padre Pio's Picture Gives me Peace

My father was the life and the soul of our family. My mother left us, so my father took care of the family for 22 years. He was very devoted to Padre Pio. After my father passed away, I found it difficult to come to terms with his death. I became so depressed that I took an overdose of sleeping pills. Two hours later, my brother and his wife found me and I was rushed to the hospital. The doctor said there was a 50/50 chance of my survival. A patient at the hospital, an elderly lady, gave me a picture of Padre Pio. I made a complete recovery and miraculously had no liver damage from the pills I took. I now pray to Padre Pio regularly and consider him my best friend. Looking at his picture, gives me a sense of peace. – Name Withheld

Devotion to Padre Pio

My husband Bob and I first learned about Padre Pio by attending a slide presentation on his life at the Immaculate Conception parish in Queens, New York. We were both very inspired by the presentation. Shortly after that, we attended the Feast Day Celebration of Our Lady of Mt. Carmel at Our Lady of Mt. Carmel parish in Brooklyn. I took my mother to the celebration in her wheelchair. It was extremely hot that day in July. I needed to get my mother out of the sun as soon as possible and into some shade. I looked everywhere but the only shady place I could see was across the street. When I walked across the street, I was surprised to see there a shrine which was dedicated to Padre Pio. Beside a beautiful and large bronze statue of Padre Pio, my mother rested and got relief from the hot sun. It was the only bit of shade in the whole area. Our devotion to Padre Pio began to grow as we learned more about him. We live in an apartment building in Forest Hills, New York which has twenty-four hour parking service. Recently, after the attendant parked our car, he introduced himself to us. His name is Daniel and he is from Poland. He told us that he noticed the picture of Padre Pio that we have on the driver's side of our car and said that he had received a miracle from Padre Pio about eighteen years previously. His mother had a great devotion to Padre Pio. When Daniel was young, he had a serious problem with his leg and needed to have surgery. His mother was so worried about his condition that she decided to go to San Giovanni Rotondo to pray at Padre Pio's tomb. When she returned to Poland, the doctor examined Daniel's leg. There was no longer any problem with it. The doctor said that in his twenty years of medical practice, he had never seen anything like it. – Clotilde and Bob Varone

The Fragrance of Beautiful Roses Filled the Air

In the beginning of the year 2000, I had a very strong desire to travel to Padre Pio's shrine in San Giovanni Rotondo. The desire to make the trip was in my thoughts constantly so I finally made plans to go at the end of October of that year. I still did not understand why I was feeling such a strong pull to go there. In early September of the same year, my grandson was diagnosed with Neuroblastoma stage four cancer. It was a very aggressive form of cancer with no known cure. He was three and a half years old at the time. We were totally devastated with this news. My grandson was living in England, I live in Dublin, Ireland. I flew to England to help look after his older sister and to be with the family. I contacted Cathy Kelly, who runs the Padre Pio Information Centre, in Victoria, London, and she very kindly allowed me to take the mitten of Padre Pio to my grandson in the hospital. I gave Cathy my passport as good faith with the understanding that she would return it to me when I returned the mitten. We had the mitten resting on my grandson's head all night, and I was begging Padre Pio to save this child. My grandson had surgery at the Royal Marsden Cancer Hospital in London. A cancerous tumor which was the size of a golf ball was removed from his brain and he was given only four months to live. He was also given chemotherapy and radiation to his brain and spine. The doctor said that if he was to survive, he would have stunted growth as a side effect of this therapy. But the doctor did not believe that he could survive. The following day, when I returned the mitten to Cathy Kelly's office, I was totally overcome with a very strong fragrance of beautiful roses, which seemed to last for ages. I was emotional and crying and wondering what was it was all about. Cathy said that it was a sign that Padre Pio had heard my prayer. I understood then that Padre Pio would look after this child. Now I had a reason to get to San Giovanni Rotondo, and while there I was up at the chapel door at 5 am when it opened and stayed at the tomb of Padre Pio until 8 am, talking to him and praying and begging him to heal our grandchild. I told Padre Pio that if our grandson recovered, I would do something for him. I really did not know at that time how I would help Padre Pio but I would find a way. When I returned from San Giovanni Rotondo, I started the Padre Pio Devotions in Malahide, Dublin, as I had promised Padre Pio that I would do something for him. At first we held the devotions in the Carmelite Monastery in Seapark, Malahide but after six years we had to move to a bigger church because of the large crowds who attended. We are now at the Sacred Heart Church, Seabury, Malahide, Dublin. We meet on the first Friday of every month. We have an organist and choir, and we start with Eucharistic Adoration, followed by Mass celebrated by Fr. Angelus, a Capuchin Priest, who blesses the people after Mass with a mitten of Padre Pio. We always have a packed Church, with 300 to 400 people in attendance, and Fr. Angelus tells us lovely stories of Padre Pio during his homily. Last September, the members of our Prayer Group bought a beautiful statue of Padre Pio in San Giovanni Rotondo. It was shipped to Dublin for our Padre Pio Devotions which have been going now for fourteen years. Every year in September, I organize a pilgrimage to Italy. I have been doing this yearly for the past fourteen years. During our trips, we have visited Rome, Assisi, Cascia, the Holy House of Loreto, Lanciano, to see the first Eucharistic Miracle, Mount St. Angelo, where St. Michael the Archangel appeared, San Giovanni Rotondo, and more. We usually have a group of around 50 people each year. In San Giovanni Rotondo, we visit all places associated with Padre Pio, his cell, his old tomb, the beautiful new tomb where his body can be seen, the friary, the hospital, and the English office, where we see a video of Padre Pio and get a blessing with some of his relics. We also visit Manopello, the shrine of the Holy Face. Our grandson is nineteen years old now and is 5ft. 11 inches tall and is in very good health. We are forever grateful to Padre Pio for this favor and for so many other favors given to our Prayer Group members over the years. It is amazing how Padre Pio gets hold of you in so many ways and gets you working for him. He got hold of me at first when I had the strong desire to visit San Giovanni Rotondo, even before I knew that my grandson was ill. I never dreamed I would organize the Padre Pio Devotions in Dublin or the pilgrimages to Italy but I really love to do this. Padre Pio makes you work hard for him. He is our great friend! – Noreen Handley

Someone was Speaking to Him, Urging Him to Make the Retreat

I have a brother who is full of anger, bitterness, resentment, hate, and selfishness. There is so much negativity in his body, mind and spirit. For two years I have been trying to get him to go on an ACTS retreat which is a wonderful Catholic four day retreat in our area in San Antonio, Texas. He finally decided to make the retreat and then two days before, on a Tuesday, my husband told me that he had changed his mind and was not going. I told my husband I was going to the computer to pray to Padre Pio and ask for his help and intercession. I went to the guestbook at saintpio.org and prayed to Padre Pio asking him to help my brother. The next day my brother had changed his mind again and had decided to go. He told me that he was sitting on his sofa at his apartment, thinking about his life, when he felt as though someone was speaking to him, urging him to make the retreat. When he returned from the four day retreat, he said that he had finally accepted Jesus into his life and he acknowledged that Jesus has always been there for him. He said that he just couldn't see it before. He is now on fire for God and sharing his faith with others. I give thanks and praise to Padre Pio, Our Lord Jesus Christ and Mother Mary. Praise God! Thank you Padre Pio! We love you. – Name Withheld

I Became a Priest for the Archdiocese of Los Angeles

I went through twelve years of Catholic schooling but after I graduated from high school I lost all interest in the Church. I still tried to do good works and to do my part to make the world a better place, but my belief in God and the value of religion was limited. Many years later, it began to dawn on me that maybe there was more to God after all and I decided to take another look at the faith I was raised in. I reasoned that if God truly existed, the Catholic Church and the Sacraments would be the best way to unite with Him. Returning to the Sacraments would allow me to be available to God's transforming power in the world. I finally made my confession after a thirteen year absence from the Church and began to attend Mass daily. I used to help my brother who was a parish priest and I assisted him in his various ministries. One day when we were driving, I noticed a picture of a saint that he had placed near the dashboard of his car. I did not know who the saint was, but the moment I looked at the picture, I started to cry. My brother told me that it was a picture of Padre Pio. I had never heard of him as I had been away from the Church for a long time. It dawned on me at that very moment that I had not made my way back to my Catholic faith on my own like I had assumed. I had alot of arrogance which was an obstacle in my path but I couldn't see it at the time. When I saw the picture of Padre Pio, I had the deep conviction that it was he who had helped me in my conversion and that he had been praying and interceding for me. More than 15 years later I entered the seminary. In 2006, after studying in the seminary for six years, I became a priest for the Archdiocese of Los Angeles and I now serve in the city of Pasadena. – Father Paul Griesgraber

A Beautiful Dream

Not long ago I had a dream in which I was driving in a car with my father. As we were driving, I told my father to stop in front of Our Lady of Sorrows parish because I wanted to go inside. Our Lady of Sorrows is a parish in my hometown of Kansas City but it is not the parish I attend. In my dream, as I entered the church, I saw a statue of a man with a brown robe and a beard. At the base of the statue were dozens of beautiful red roses. There was a kneeler in front of the statue and so I knelt down. The statue then spoke to me, teaching me how to pray. It was the most beautiful dream I have ever had in my life. I often though about the statue and wondered who it was. At Christmas, I received a book about Padre Pio and when I saw a picture of a statue of Padre Pio it was exactly like the one in my dream. Knowing that Padre Pio is helping me in my journey through life is a great consolation. – Michael Feierabend

Padre Pio's Glove was Placed on my Husband

In 1994, my husband became very ill with Crohn's Disease. He was not responding to the medical treatment that he was given. He became sicker and sicker and was in the Maine General Hospital in Waterville, Maine for 45 days. He had lost so much weight that he looked like a skeleton. There was a Padre Pio prayer group that met at St. Mary's parish in Agusta and my friend contacted them and told them about my husband's condition. They gave her their relic to borrow. It was a part of Padre Pio's glove encased in glass. They promised to pray for my husband. I brought the relic to the hospital that night and placed it on my husband's stomach and he and I prayed the novena to the Sacred Heart of Jesus. That was the prayer that Padre Pio had always prayed. My husband called me from the hospital at 4:00 a.m. the next morning. I was surprised since he was so weak that he could barely lift his hand. He told me that something had happened when the glove was placed on his stomach. He felt a warmth go all the way through his body. When the doctors came in to examine him the next morning, they were astounded. The swelling in his stomach had disappeared. They decided to go ahead and do surgery but the surgery went beautifully and he has never been bothered with this dread disease since. I know Padre Pio's powerful intercession healed my husband and it was after that experience that I became a spiritual child of Padre Pio. – Ann Douglass

A Visit

I first saw Padre Pio in 1964 when my late husband and I were on pilgrimage. The first morning we attended his Mass, we were fortunate to sit on a side pew next to the altar and were able to observe him closely. Somehow I could see the heavy cross on his shoulder and I could not ask for any favors as I felt he would have to suffer still more to obtain a favor for me. However, I wanted my Rosary blessed. After Mass, the men gathered in another room to get Padre Pio's blessing. I gave my Rosary to my husband and I knelt by the altar and in my prayer asked Padre Pio to bless my Rosary. When my husband returned I could see that he was visibly shaken. He said that Padre Pio was walking around the room from one man to the next and when he came to the opposite side of the room, he quickly turned around and walked straight up to my husband and placed his hand on my Rosary. My husband said that Padre Pio's penetrating look into his eyes made his eyes almost hurt. – Mrs. Carl Blasingame

Your Healing Will Come

I often spent my time praying before a crucifix that is in my parish church. One night I had a dream in which I saw Padre Pio. Two Capuchin priests were with him and they were all standing in a church, in front of the tabernacle. In my dream, Padre Pio pointed at the tabernacle and told me that my healing was going to come but it would come from the Blessed Sacrament. Since then, I always spend time in adoration of the Blessed Sacrament. Shortly afterward, I had an operation and it was very successful. I pray to Padre Pio every day of my life, beginning with his chaplet and the Novena to the Sacred Heart of Jesus which he prayed daily. – Nicoline Kenjing

In Quezon City, Philippines, I Found a Prayer Pamphlet

In the year 2000, 3 months after our wedding, we learned that my wife was pregnant. Like other newly-wed couples, we were extremely delighted with the news. Thursday of that week, my wife went to the doctor. That day was a most difficult day for us as the doctor told us that she suspected an ectopic pregnancy. A sonogram revealed that it was indeed true. The baby was growing in the fallopian tube instead of the uterus. We were devastated by the news. We decided to go to another clinic and have another sonogram done, just to be sure. The second sonogram revealed the same. We returned to my wife's doctor who informed us that the pregnancy had to be terminated. The baby could not survive and my wife's life was endangered as well. The doctor wanted to schedule the procedure for Monday. Before we went home that day, we visited the Our Lady of Lourdes Church in Quezon City, Philippines. We prayed so hard hoping that a miracle would happen. As I was praying, I noticed a little prayer pamphlet in the church. It was a pamphlet about Padre Pio, with prayers and devotions. I had never heard of Padre Pio before. I showed the pamphlet to my wife and told her that we should pray and seek Padre Pio's intercession. We prayed to Padre Pio for the safety of our little one. We prayed that the baby would move towards the uterus. I began to feel confident that everything would be fine. Monday came and we postponed the procedure to terminate the preganancy. I went to work and shared our predicament with close friends. My Godmother told me to seek another opinion. We went to the doctor she recommended to us. He told us to postpone the procedure for one month and to continue to pray. After a prayerful month, we learned that the baby had moved towards the uterus. We received an answer to our prayers through the intercession of Padre Pio! Our first born child is a healthy 9 year old boy now. He is doing very well in school and is turning out to be a fine boy. His name is Pio! I thank God for letting us experience His presence in our family through St. Padre Pio. Today, we continue to pray and seek Padre Pio's intercession for guidance. –Mike Cunanan

Free of Cigarette Addiction

I visited the Padre Pio friary in Salcete, in Goa, India and became acquainted with Brother Peter, OFM Cap. He is one of the Franciscans who lives in the friary. The friary in Salcete is about a three hour distance from where I live in Siolim, Goa, India. I was able to visit the chapel in the friary that is dedicated to Padre Pio. Brother Peter, who is ninety-eight years old, gave me a prayer for the intercession of Padre Pio and after having the prayer for a number of months, I finally started to say the novena to Padre Pio. I prayed to be able to quit smoking and thanks be to God, my prayer was answered. After being a smoker for twenty-two years, on March 18, 2007, I was healed of my addiction to cigarettes. Padre Pio has helped me in other difficulties as well and is working wonders in my life and in my family's life. – Ballerina Martins Pinto

An Unusual Fragrance

I suffered from a sharp pain in my rib cage for four months. The pain was so severe that it became even painful to breathe. I went to the emergency room and had further tests and doctor visits but the cause remained a mystery. One day, in the mail, I received a little medal of Padre Pio. I pinned it on my shirt and right after that, the pain left and has never returned. A short time later, I woke up from a sound sleep to a very unusual and sweet fragrance that was in my bedroom. I do not use perfume so I could not understand what it was. The next morning, as soon as I woke up, I noticed the Padre Pio newsletter, "Pray, Hope, and Don't Worry" on my table. I had picked it up at church. The title of the newsletter was, "The Extraordinary Perfume of Padre Pio." I read the story about Padre Pio's perfume and then I understood. Thank you, St. Pio. Never in my wildest dreams would I have thought that your spirit would visit me in such a way. – Angie Delarosa

The Doctor was Perplexed

I have a friend named Glenda who is a Protestant and belongs to the Presbyterian denomination. I shared with her the prayers of Padre Pio and told her about his life and his familiar saying, "Pray, Hope, and Don't Worry." I gave her a Padre Pio Rosary. I also gave her a pamphlet on how to pray the Rosary and suggested that she pray it each day. Glenda thought it was a good idea and began to pray the Rosary every morning. She told me that whenever she had entered a Catholic Church in the past, she always had a special feeling. I told her that she was feeling the real presence of Jesus in the Blessed Sacrament. Glenda had to go to the hospital for quadruple bypass heart surgery. Her sister called me to let me know that she came through the surgery just fine. However, her sister said that the doctor had come to her room the next day and he was perplexed. He told Glenda that she was repeating some initials during the operation and he as well as all of the doctors and nurses who were attending her, were curious as to what she was saying. He said that none of his patients had ever murmured even one word during open heart surgery. The anesthetic they are given is so strong, that they do not utter a sound in their unconscious state. But Glenda for some reason, was different. "What was I saying?" Glenda asked him. "You were constantly repeating the initials, P, H, D, W the doctor answered. We would like to know what it stand for. Then Glenda understood and told him, "It stands for "Pray, Hope, and Don't Worry." The doctor has since shared the phrase with his patients who are preparing for surgery. – Tom Thurston

My Mother and Sister Prayed to Padre Pio for me

I am a sixteen year old girl suffering from a terrible disease known as Anorexia Nervosa, a disease where the person thinks he/she is fat and refuses to eat. I started getting some treatment last September. At that time, I was in a pretty bad way. I denied I had a problem, would eat only very small amounts of food, and was terrified at the thought of putting on weight and getting fat. My mother, sister, and close relations were praying to Padre Pio for me. Thankfully in December I started to pull myself together. I started to eat more and to follow the doctors' orders. The weight went up in tiny amounts and I began to look and feel better. Around the month of March I began praying to Padre Pio myself, asking him for his help. Since then things have been going great. Thankfully I've nearly reached my target weight and soon, thanks to Padre Pio, I hope to be living a normal, healthy life once more, enabling me to make those terrible few months a thing of the past. – Patricia Walsh

Today I Am Not Alone

I was in very rough shape before I came across the compassion and miracles of Padre Pio, being very ill myself with many complications due to chronic Lyme disease. I suffer from seizures, joint problems, and days when I cannot get out of bed due to pain. This illness cost me my job, my savings, and my car. I am also taking care of my 84 year old aunt, who has diabetes and emphysema, and pain in virtually every joint due to arthritis. But worst of all, was the daily feeling I had of being a "failure" based upon a past of making many poor decisions. I was filled with fear, worry, and other forms of errors and sins. I had no idea what it might be like to actually feel like a good person. No matter what I did (and I was a nurse and a volunteer for many causes) I felt I was very alone in this world. Other than my aunt, my family is gone. No matter how many prayers I prayed, it never seemed to help. There were days when I felt it would be best if I was not here. A few weeks ago, a Christian magazine came to my home, and in it was a story about a teenager who had a life-threatening accident. His mother was given a prayer card of Padre Pio. She prayed to Padre Pio and miraculously, her son began to recover. I had never heard of Padre Pio so I started researching him at the library and on the internet. I learned about this holy saint of compassion and kindness, and I dared to try one more prayer, to ask him for healing and help. On my way home from the library, I walked past the usual homes and noticed the scent of flowers that I could not place. There were no blooms in the yards I was passing. In fact, all that was nearby was a gas line. I felt the presence o f a warm stranger walking with me but there was no one there. I am sure it was Padre Pio. Today, I am not alone. Today, I have no pain. Today, I feel that I am loved, and I receive help with my many cares. Thank you, St. Pio! – Mari Rusnak

I Was Very Worried About my Son

I was half out of my mind with worry over my oldest son who was in the Air Force flying helicopters. I would cry and cry and walk the floor. Then I heard about Padre Pio. I wrote to him, begging him to pray so that my son would be safe. I received a letter from Italy saying that Padre Pio would pray for me. It was just about the time he would have received my letter, that I changed completely. I didn't worry about my son anymore or cry. I was a different person. And needless to say, my son came home safe. – Eileen Dunham

I Was Given the Last Rites

In September 2004 I spent two months in the hospital and was placed on life support. I was the victim of a shooting. Several times during the operation to remove the bullet, my heart stopped. My family asked the doctor to tell them the truth about my condition. The doctor said that I had a three percent chance of surviving. A priest came in the hospital and gave me the Last Rites. When I came back to consciousness, I was in excruciating pain. I was so weak that I could not even lift my head up from the pillow or raise my arms or legs. I have a very big family and for the two months I was in the hospital, they never left my bedside. My family prayed to Padre Pio, asking for his intercession so that my life would be spared. One of his relics was placed on me. I slowly began to get better. When the doctors saw the improvement they called me a "living miracle." They told me that they had given up hope for my recovery. I believe that I am alive today and back to normal because of the intercession of Padre Pio. I truly believe Padre Pio gave me back my life. – Name Withheld

I Have Prepared Her Death Certificate

I learned about Padre Pio through a lady named Judy Hayes. Judy shared with me some of the incidents of St. Pio's life. She told me that she had received a miracle by praying to him. From that time forward I have had a great devotion to Padre Pio. When Judy learned that she had cancer, it was already in stage four and had spread to her bones. She went to a religious articles store to get a novena to pray for healing. While there, she noticed a holy card of Padre Pio. It seemed to be calling to her. Judy bought the Padre Pio prayer card and began to pray to him for his intercession. She prayed that she might be healed of cancer. Shortly after that, she had a health crisis and had to go to the hospital for several months. While in the hospital, Judy overheard the nurse talking to the other nurses. The nurse said, "Judy's condition is so bad that she will die tonight. I have already prepared her death certificate. It needs to be given to the doctor for his signature." What the nurse did not know was that Judy was praying to St. Pio for healing. She is alive today and cancer-free. I thank God for St. Pio and for the help I have received from him in my own life. – Kathleen Lusk

A Marriage in Trouble

My wife and I had been married for three years. I thought she was the woman of my life and I loved her desperately. One day I met a person who made me have doubts about my marriage. It was as if the devil was working against me. I prayed to God and to Padre Pio to free me from this horrible situation as my mind was out of control. I kept trying to avoid the person, but even if I kept away, the thought was constantly in my mind. I decided to talk to a priest about my problem. He told me to keep praying to the Lord and to my dear Padre Pio because there are moments in time when everything feels lost. All the things you believe in seem to be lies. I managed to overcome that episode, considering it one of the many challenges in life which I was able to face thanks to my dear Padre Pio. – Name Withheld

A Novena to Padre Pio

In May, 1995, false charges were brought against me and I was suspended from my work until the investigation was completed. I was really shaken up and my wife and children were also very upset. Then, my friend gave me a copy of the prayer that Padre Pio used to say and she asked me to make a novena. As I am not Catholic, I did not know how to make a novena. She explained it to and I started saying this prayer. After a few days, my wife and I were seated in front of our cottage. It was a beautiful day and suddenly we saw a rainbow far in the distance. As we watched this beautiful sight, to our astonishment, the far end of the rainbow advanced toward us. It finally stopped directly in front of us, dancing in the lake. We were astounded. All at once, I knew that this was an answer to the prayer that I had made through the intervention of Padre Pio. The following week I received a letter from my employer that the investigation had been completed, and that I was found not guilty of the charges. At this point I am a Protestant, amazed at the power of this prayer, and very thankful to God and to Padre Pio for having interceded on my behalf. – Name Withheld

I Told Her to Touch Each Bead and Say "Jesus I Love You"

About 3 years ago my niece, Patricia Gail was diagnosed with thymus cancer. She was told to get her affairs in order and to make provisions to have someone take care of her two children, for she did not have much time left. Gail is not a practicing Christian, but she does believe in Jesus as her Savior. I worked at a Catholic Book & Gift Shop and bought her a St. Padre Pio Rosary, had it blessed and took it to the hospital to give to her. I told her about St. Pio and the many healings that occurred through him. She informed me that she was not Catholic and did not know how to pray the Rosary. Her surgery was the next day and time was a factor so I told her just to touch each bead and say, "Jesus, I love You." After the surgery, the doctor came to the waiting room and said that he removed all of the tumor. He said that it looked to be cancer and the blood work showed it to be cancer and that she would most likely need to have chemo-therapy. At least ten days went by and Gail was so surprised at the results of the lab work. The tumor was not cancerous and she was healed. Gail was told that she was a miracle. I even heard her state that she was a miracle. I thank God for the gift of believing and seeing with my soul His marvelous miracles and feeling His comforting love. – Kathy Bee

Padre Pio Led me Back to God

Five years ago I had fallen away from the church. I had become an alcoholic and I was also going around with a married man. My mother, father and family who are devout Catholics tried their very best with me but I did not want anybody telling me what to do. One day my sister gave me a picture of Padre Pio and a little novena prayer. I was always going to say the prayer "tomorrow." It was the same with going to church, always tomorrow. But tomorrow never came. I put the picture of Padre Pio in a drawer and every time I opened the drawer I saw Padre Pio. Eventually, the picture seemed to be always in my mind. The day I said the novena changed my life. I felt that I wanted to go back to church and to pray. Padre Pio led me back to almighty God and his Blessed Mother. – Name Withheld

I Shed Tears at Padre Pio's Mass

Padre Pio staggered forward on his stigmatized feet onto the altar where Our Blessed Lady accompanied him every morning for his Mass. The church was packed every morning with approximately 2,000 people. You realized that there were also 2,000 guardian angels in that church. One morning, during the month of October 1960, I arrived outside the entrance to the church to take my place in the queue, awaiting the opening of the doors. I counted 50 separate buses bringing people to the Mass. That didn't include people walking from the town of San Giovanni Rotondo. Padre Pio prayed, begged and pleaded during his Mass to relieve Jesus of his sufferings and to take on those sufferings. Sometimes when the sins of the world were revealed to him during his Mass, he would cry and he would have to make use of what was known as a "tear cloth" or a towel to wipe his eyes. He was begging and pleading all the time to relieve Jesus of his suffering. Occasionally he spoke in a language which I didn't understand. His Masses were very moving. I cried and shed tears looking at him suffering. I cried profusely morning after morning. I felt totally and utterly unworthy to be in his presence. I also felt it was my sins, and the sins of people like me, that caused Padre Pio to suffer. It also made me realize that Jesus died on the cross for my sins and for the salvation of our souls. – Donald Enright

Two Brushes with Death and Padre Pio's Intercession

On March 6, 2003, I suffered a near fatal accident when I fell down some basement stairs in a friend's house. I was taken to the Nassau University Medical Center in East Meadow, New York. I suffered three fractures to my spine as well as severe brain trauma. I became comatose. The doctors told my family that I had very little chance of survival. My mother, who lives in Florida, has had a great devotion to Padre Pio for as long as I can remember. She has a small relic of Padre Pio, a piece of his habit. She took the relic and taped it to a photograph of me. She began a prayer vigil, and through the night prayed to Padre Pio, asking for his intercession. The morning after my mother's prayer vigil, I awoke from the coma which I had been in for eleven days. Still, the doctors were not optimistic. They only gave me a fifty-fifty chance of recovery. I remained in the Intensive Care Unit of the hospital for twenty-one days. But I continued to make steady progress and finally was released from the hospital. On one of my follow-up appointments at the hospital, I ran into some of the doctors who worked in the Intensive Care Unit. My memory of them naturally was a little hazy but they recognized me because they had treated me. I greeted them and they stared at me with incredulous expressions on their faces. The senior doctor said, "Look at you, walking and talking! You are the miracle man!" I almost wept when the doctor said that to me. I learned that "miracle man" was the nickname that the hospital staff had given me. In December of the same year, an elderly woman, who had an epileptic seizure while driving, ran into my car head on. My car rolled over four times and finally landed on its side. The woman who was driving the car behind me told me that she was convinced that she was about to crash into my car as well. She said that she had lost control of her car but at the very last second, her car simply turned of its own accord, and she missed hitting me by inches. These experiences, these near brushes with death, changed me completely. I used to be a non-practicing Catholic, living in sin, going to Mass on Christmas and Easter only. I have now returned to the Catholic Church in earnest. I work as a film maker, and have worked in all aspects of the film industry. I hope to make a full-length feature film on the life of St. Pio. I carry his relic with me now at all times. I may be called the miracle man by the doctors, but we all know who the real miracle man is! From the bottom of my heart, thank you St. Pio for not losing faith in this sinner. – Peter D. Bove

I Felt that Padre Pio Wanted to be my Friend

In 2013 I was taking a course for priests in Rome and during the half term break I was wondering what I should do. To my surprise I heard a voice inside of me say, "Come to San Giovanni Rotondo." I wondered why I should go there since I have no devotion to Padre Pio. I wasn't at all interested in him. All the stories about him simply turned me off. However, again I felt something inviting me to visit the shrine. So I booked my ticket. I met two Filipino priests on the bus from Rome who took me around the shrine and monastery. My time in San Giovanni Rotondo was one pleasant experience after another. I even experienced a miracle of my own while staying there. I was suffering from terrible blisters on the soles of my feet that had been there for a week or more. I decided to go to the hospital near the shrine and I asked the nursing staff there to treat the blisters. They agreed to do so. I told them that I first had to go over to the church to say Mass but would return directly after that. When I went back to the Emergency Department after the Mass, the place was full of sick people and the nurses told me to come back the next morning. My feet were really hurting and I thought that perhaps I should have had them treated instead of going to Mass. I decided to go to confession and then I prayed at the tomb of Padre Pio. I finally went back to my room, taking a last look at my feet before I went to bed. My blisters were very bad and I could see blood in them. In the morning when I got up, the blisters were gone, my feet were healed. I was surprised. I didn't go back to the hospital but went to Mass and then prayed the Rosary. As I reflected on the life of Padre Pio I began to realize how much he must have suffered yet he trusted in God. My attitude towards him changed. He was no longer some distant Italian holy man who everybody raved about and exaggerated about. He was a real person to me and I felt I had a strong connection with him. I felt that he wanted to accompany me in my life. At the end of my three day stay in San Giovanni Rotondo, I made a final visit to church. I noticed a statue of Padre Pio on the side of the church with his arms outstretched towards the congregation. As I approached, I also noticed the saint was smiling. I felt he was looking at me. I looked at him and raised my two thumbs up and said, "Thank you, Padre Pio. This has been a wonderful experience. Thank you, thank you!" I look back on my trip to the shrine with gratitude. It was a divine invitation, that I am sure. I feel that Padre Pio wanted to be my friend and I feel he wants to help me. I believe he lead me to a closer relationship with Jesus and the words of the holy man, "pray, hope, and don't worry" remind me to trust all the more in our loving and merciful Savior. – Father Joseph Colby

She Will be Drawing Water from the Well

Padre Pio is no stranger to my family. In the 1950's, my cousin Sara wanted desperately to become a nun but could not leave home because of her mother Rosa's very poor health. Sara was taking care of her and she did not feel she could leave her to enter the convent. She wanted to talk to Padre Pio about it so she contacted San Giovanni Rotondo and then she and her father traveled by train from their home in Sant' Alfio, Sicily to speak to him. During the train ride, Sara and her father had something to eat. During the meal, her father accidently spilled some wine on his clothing. Sara felt very embarrassed to think that Padre Pio might see the wine stains on her father's clothing or even worse that they would greet Padre Pio with her father smelling of wine. She gave her father a scolding. When they finally were able to speak to Padre Pio, he assured her that she would be able to enter the convent and that her mother would be fine. In fact, Padre Pio told them that upon their return home, they would find Rosa drawing water from the well. This was impossible for her to do since she suffered from serious heart problems and was too weak to perform even the simplest and most menial tasks. During their conversation, Padre Pio told Sara not to ever again scold her father. My cousin was shocked that Padre Pio knew that this had happened on the train. Needless to say, when they returned home, they found Rosa drawing water from the well just as Padre Pio assured them. Rosa regained her health immediately and miraculously. Sara was able to leave home and enter the convent. I am also proud to say that I have experienced Padre Pio's love and intercession in my own life and also with my immediate family. We too have received many graces through the intercession of Padre Pio. – Rosa Del Popolo

Your Son is in Poland

I was made a prisoner by the Germans on September 18, 1943 and sent to concentration camps, first in Austria, then in Eastern Prussia. In March 1944, I was sent to Camp 307 at Deblin in Poland. It was then that my mother went to see Padre Pio for she had no news of me and heard on the radio that many Italian officers had been shot. . . .Padre Pio came up to my mother after Mass and, touching her on the head, exclaimed, "Your son Pompeo is in Poland, a prisoner. He is in good health but he is tightening his belt (he is suffering hunger)." Later my mother went to confession and she was surprised to hear Padre Pio repeat the words: "Your son Pompeo is a prisoner. You'll have news soon." After passing through various camps in Germany and Holland, I got home in 1945. My mother then told me of her visit to Padre Pio.

When I returned to Italy, I was asked by a journalist, "What has remained with you after all those sorrowful experiences?" "The faith," I replied. – Pompeo Querques

A Bicycle Accident

I have a strong devotion to Padre Pio and have prayed that he would accept me as one of his spiritual children. Not long ago I had a very serious mountain biking accident in which I broke 5 of my ribs and punctured my lung. My accident occurred in a valley which was about 45 minutes away from the nearest road. There was no one nearby to help me. I could barely breathe and I was choking on my blood. I felt like I was dying. I thought of my family and I wanted to live so that I could take care of them. I began to pray to Padre Pio and the Blessed Virgin Mary to help me. Although still in pain, after praying to Padre Pio and the Virgin Mary, I was able to breathe much easier and the bleeding subsided. It took over an hour for the paramedics to arrive and then I was life-flighted to the hospital. I believe without the help of Padre Pio and the Blessed Mother Mary I would not have made it out of that valley alive. Thank you Padre Pio and our Holy Mother in Heaven. – Caterina Brott

A Transformation in My Life

I am 20 years old and a student of the University for Development Studies in Ghana, West Africa. I recently read about Padre Pio on the website and listened to his voice and read the many testimonials recorded. My heart was so touched by what I read. I began to pray his "Prayer after Holy Communion" every day. Since then, I have seen a transformation in my life, morally, socially, and even academically. – Ayinbora Joshua

The Room was Filled with the Fragrance of Violets

After the birth of my third child, I suffered a post partum depression which affected me with phobias that made me ill and in many ways made me incapable of caring for my infant and the family. I had heard all about Fr. Pio from a relative of mine. I had written to Fr. Pio about my plight and asked for his intercession. His superior wrote back to me saying, "Fr. Pio wants you to know that all will be well." Shortly after that as I prayed before a picture of Fr. Pio, I sensed his presence and the room was filled with the fragrance of violets. From that moment on, I was cured of this ailment. – Name Withheld

A Child's Healing

My daughter Margaret, who was born in 1950, had always been weak and ill. I had taken her to several doctors and they said that she would grow out of it. A doctor came to her school and upon seeing Margaret he sent me a letter stating that I should take her to a heart specialist. She was eleven years old at the time. When she was examined and x-rayed, it was found that she had a hole in her heart and the valves in her heart were small. She would have to have a serious operation but since she was so weak she was sent home to build up her strength for the surgery. When we came home, Margaret told me she would write a letter to Padre Pio. She did this and a short time later she received a nice letter from him. He told her not to worry but to go the hospital and everything would be all right. When we went to the doctor and another x-ray was taken, the doctor asked me what had been done to her. I told him nothing for I did not know what he was talking about. He showed me both x-ray's. One showed a large hole in the heart and the last x-ray showed that the hole was almost closed. She didn't have to go in for the heart operation. – Mary Cunningham

Padre Pio Pressed my Crucifix to His Lips

I visited San Giovanni Rotondo and attended Padre Pio's Mass several times, when as a U.S. soldier, I was stationed in Italy during World War II. The first time I met Padre Pio, I was very nervous and shaking in my boots. However, he smiled at me when we were introduced, and I lost all of my fear. Because I did not speak Italian, one of the Capuchins acted as translator. Padre Pio was very friendly and seemed happy to greet me. He had a wonderful sense of humor and often liked to tell innocent jokes. On several occasions, the other soldiers and I would walk with Padre Pio down the hall when he was on his way to hear the mens' confessions. One time I asked him to bless a crucifix of mine. He took it and blessed it and then pressed it to his lips very hard before giving it back to me. Mary Pyle, his secretary, told me many things about Padre Pio's life. She was a third order Franciscan and had a house just below the monastery. After Padre Pio's Sunday Mass, a group of soldiers and I would visit Mary and she would serve us breakfast. I also met Padre Pio's father at Mary Pyle's house. He was a quiet man and I remember that he was able to speak some English. After the war was over and I returned to the U.S. Mary and I kept in touch through letters. When Mary and a friend of her's came on a visit to the U.S. they visited me in Philadelphia. – Joe Revelas

I Put a Picture of Padre Pio in my Granddaughter's Incubator

My daughter Nicole was pregnant with identical twin girls and had a medical crisis. Her due date was Sept. 24, 2011. On Sunday, June 19, 2011, my daughter was feeling significant pain in her side and called her doctor to advise him. The doctor told her it was probably the twins resting on a nerve but scheduled an appointment for that Wednesday, June 22. The doctor examined Nicole and said that everything appeared to be fine but decided to do a sonogram. The sonogram indicated that one baby had too much fluid. This condition is called TTTS (twin to twin transfusion syndrome). They rushed Nicole to the hospital and she was met by a team of doctors. The doctors said she was in a stage 4 condition of TTTS which is very serious. The twins had slight heart beats and the doctors suggested the following options to my daughter: A) Cut the umbilical cord of baby Taylor, the twin with too much fluid. Taylor would then die but possibly baby Alexa would survive. B) Take no action and at some point both babies would die. C) Deliver the babies immediately although there was no guarantee that they would live. My daughter had just a few minutes to make a decision and she chose option C and both babies were delivered via an emergency C-Section at Winthrop Hospital in Mineola, New York. The twins were delivered at 26 ½ weeks and a few minutes after birth were given the Apgar test which tells the general health of the newborn. The score is from one to ten, one being the lowest. Taylor received a score of one and medically had no chance of survival. Alexa was given a two to three score and had a slightly better chance of survival. While this was happening I received a call that the twins were dying and that I should leave my hair salon business and come immediately to the hospital. While driving to the hospital, which was forty-five minutes away, I prayed and cried, asking the Lord to save the twins. I felt in my heart that the Holy Spirit was speaking to me saying that they would survive. It took seventeen minutes to stabilize Taylor who was in grave danger and then both babies were placed in two separate incubators. I was surrounded by bad news for days so I took a picture of St. Pio's bleeding hands and put it in the incubator with Taylor who was in critical condition. Alexa was in stable but critical condition. I had a strong desire to put a picture of Blessed John Paul II in the incubator as well. I had a 5 by 7 plaque at home of John Paul II but it was too big to put in the incubator. I asked my sister and family and friends if anyone had a smaller picture of him but I had no success in finding one. At this point I asked the Lord for His will to be done and prayed to St. Pio and Blessed John Paul II to intercede. A week went by and one of my customers came into the hair salon. He was seventeen years old and told me he had just returned from Rome and while praying in front of the tomb of John Paul II he felt led to get a picture of him and a medal and bring it to me. The young man said he didn't understand it but he knew he had to do it. I put the picture in Taylor's incubator and the rest was in God's hands. The twins are now four years old and weight over thirty-five pounds and are both in good health. We are not sure which doctor or nurse placed this on Taylor's crib, but the morning of discharge from the NICU (neonatal intensive care unit) there was a Certificate of Excellency on Taylor's crib that read, "Taylor Walker, 114 days in the NICU- A True Miracle." – Mr. Raffaele Ferraioli

I was Able to Forgive my Father

I have been praying to Padre Pio for my health as I have been unwell lately but I think he interceded for me in a different way than I had envisioned. I had issues with my father for most of my life. He had been a difficult person to live with and many times he was aggressive to me and to my mother. I could not understand why she stayed with him and put up with it. When he was hospitalized a few weeks ago, I did not go to see him as I still felt a lot of anger toward him for what had happened between us. When his condition became worse, I was told that he might not have long to live. My mother was there at his bedside and I felt that I should go to the hospital for her sake and to support her. When I got to the hospital, I was shocked at my father's serious condition. I felt that I needed to pray to Padre Pio for him. That evening when I returned home, I continued to pray to Padre Pio. The next day my father was much worse and was now unconscious. I asked Padre Pio to intercede so that my father would not suffer but would have a peaceful death. What is amazing is that during that time my anger totally disappeared and I was able to fully forgive my father and also to ask for forgiveness for some of the things I had said to him when he was alive. I was able to hold his hand as he died and he was very peaceful and calm. I believe that this was all due to the intercession of the blessed Padre Pio whom I have been long devoted to. I want to thank Padre Pio again and to let others know of this. I never thought I could forgive my father but I now feel at peace with him. – Francesca

The Catholic Chaplain Prayed for my Wife

My wife was diagnosed with a terminal brain tumor. As part of her treatment, the doctor surgically inserted a VP shunt into the ventricle in her brain. At one point, she was rushed to UCSD Hospital (La Jolla, CA) because the shunt had stopped working properly. In the emergency room, she could only respond to me by pressing my hand. The doctor had already told me that the prognosis for my wife was not good. One day while walking towards her room, I stepped on a piece of paper and when I picked it up, I discovered that it was a prayer pamphlet of Padre Pio. Right after I picked up the prayer card of Padre Pio, I happened to see the Catholic chaplain who was making his morning rounds at the hospital. I asked him if he would pray for my wife and I showed him the prayer of Padre Pio that I had just picked up off the floor. The priest immediately asked a nurse for a safety pin. He walked to my wife's room with me and pinned the prayer card to her hospital gown and then said a prayer for her healing and comfort. My wife's condition suddenly made a turn from worst to good. That was three years ago, and as for now, my wife's brain cancer is stable. It is still there but it is not growing. The doctor's prognosis gave her only one year to live. Again thank you Blessed St. Father Pio for your blessing and may you continue to watch over my wife. – Joseph Lagos

I Can Now Live a Normal Life

I had been suffering from a fear of closed places and big department stores and had not the courage to walk across the street or even to walk my dog for more than 5 minutes without some other person being with me. I was also afraid to drive alone in my car for fear of fainting. Last year while on holiday at my parents' home, I received from my mother a simple prayer to Padre Pio with a photo of him. Immediately after seeing the photo I felt that if any one person living or dead could help me, then it would be Padre Pio. After one and a half years of being afraid to go shopping, drive my car alone, or walk alone, I suddenly lost my fears and can now live once again my normal life with my wife and children. – N.C. Holmes

I Prayed that My Mother Would Receive the Last Rites

My mother was diagnosed with Parkinson's disease. The most painful part of the illness for her was the awareness that she was losing her independence and her sharpness of mind. After four years, my sisters and I realized that she could no longer remain in her own home, even with 24-hour care. We found a lovely care facility for her. Mom's condition rapidly worsened. During this time, I prayed daily to Padre Pio that Mom would have a priest to assist her and give her the Last Rites before she passed away. I begged Padre Pio to help her in this way. After a fall, she was moved to a hospital and her condition worsened. However, when Fr. Don came to see her, she recognized and remembered him and was able to receive the sacraments of Anointing of the sick and the Eucharist. Two days later, I received a call that I needed to come to her bedside to say goodbye. I called her and told her I was on my way. She had not been able to have a phone conversation for 6 months. But she was able to take my call and to understand what I was saying to her. As I hung up the phone, the scent of roses filled the car. I thanked Padre Pio for obtaining these favors for me and for my mother. She passed away peacefully two days later. Glory to God for his tremendous prayer warrior, Padre Pio. – Kayte Russell

I Asked Padre Pio to Send Me a Sign

A few years ago I was praying to St. Pio and I asked him to send me a sign that he was listening to my prayers. Well, about a week later I received a package in the mail from Italy. The package came from San Giovanni Rotondo. A letter inside the package informed me that I had won the "Epiphany Raffle." I had never even heard of the Epiphany Raffle. I won books on St. Pio, a number of beautiful photographs of St. Pio, a St. Pio hat and many other St. Pio items. Padre Pio had given me his sign that he was definitely listening to my prayers. – Josie Grossi

Brenda, You Had Better Get Up!

Once, while on a job-hunting trip, I checked into a motel for the night. Several people who were at the motel made me feel uneasy. I began to feel a concern for the safety of my car and I hoped that it would not be vandalized in the night. Before I went to bed, I prayed and asked Padre Pio to watch over me and protect me and also my car. That night,I had a dream. In the dream, I was laying on my right side, and Padre Pio came and shook me awake saying, "Brenda, I think you'd better get up now." When I woke up, I was laying on my right side, just like in my dream. I looked at the clock and saw that it was 3:00 a.m. I was so groggy, that I fell asleep again. I then had a second dream in which Padre Pio shook me once again, saying with greater emphasis, "Brenda! You had better get up now!" At that, I got up and looked out the window. Sure enough, the two fellows who had concerned me after I checked in to the motel, were at my car. One of them was under it! They left hastily when that saw me at the window. I am convinced that Padre Pio heard my prayer that night and came to my rescue. – Brenda Zizzo

Lord, Send Padre Pio to Help my Parents

In my younger years, when I was on a quest to grow in spiritual understanding, I found a used book, a biography of Padre Pio. After I read the book, I knew that I wanted Padre Pio to be my spiritual father for the rest of my life. Many years later, I read another book on his life and my dedication to him grew even greater. When my mother and father were in their early 80's, they were having some financial difficulties. One night I knelt by my bed and prayed, "Lord, send Padre Pio to my parents to help them." Two weeks later, I was visiting my parents when my mother said, "I had a most unusual experience a few nights ago. I woke up at 3:00 a.m. and there was a monk standing right next to me. The hood of his habit was pulled up on his head." I asked my mother if she was afraid and she told me that she had no fear at all. On the contrary, she said that she felt very peaceful. When the monk appeared at her bedside, she looked over at my father because she intended to wake him up, and when she looked back, the monk was gone. I then told her that I had prayed to Padre Pio and I had asked him to help both her and my father. Right after that, my parents' financial difficulties all resolved and they had no more worries. I believe that my parents realized that Padre Pio's visit was an answer to my prayers. But because they were both Protestants, and because the idea of saints was not in their religious tradition, I feel that they had some difficulty comprehending what had happened. Through the years, the blessings that I have received from Padre Pio continue to help me and to strengthen my faith in God. – Dr. Ron Cobb – Retired Colonel, U.S. Army

Padre Pio said, "I Love the Filippinos"

I did not know God nor go to church regularly, nor even pray the Rosary. My visit to Padre Pio's monastery in San Giovanni Rotondo changed my whole life and brought me very close to God. Also, Father Odon Santos, P.P. of Magalang used to speak to us about the wonders and miracles he saw with his own eyes when on a visit to Padre Pio. The day after Father Santos arrived in San Giovanni Rotondo, while with a group of priests, Padre Pio called him aside and said to him, "You are a priest from the Philippines. I love the Filippinos!" Padre Pio asked Father Santos to offer Mass at his altar and to use his vestments. Father Santos was overcome with joy. – Eusebio Lopez

I Have Been Feeling Much, Much Better

I have been suffering from depression off and on for three years since the death of my husband and I would like you to know since I have been praying to Padre Pio to intercede for me and I have been feeling much, much better. – Name withheld

My Father's Dream

My father, Italo Francia had not been feeling well. When he went to the doctor for tests, it was found that he had a large cancerous tumor. In order to shrink the tumor, he was given radiation and chemotherapy at the Metropolitan Hospital's Windsor Cancer Center in Windsor, Ontario, Canada. After that, he had surgery. He had to continue with the chemotherapy treatments after the surgery. The treatments made him so ill that he said that he would rather die than endure any more of them. He told his doctor that he had decided to discontinue the treatments. My mother and I resigned ourselves to my father's decision. Throughout my father's illness, my mother had been praying to Padre Pio for a cure. I too prayed for Padre Pio's intercession. I pulled out an old prayer card that my mother had given me years before. I prayed to Padre Pio that my father would be healed and that he would be able to walk me, his only daughter, down the aisle some day. If however, it was his time to die, I prayed that he would not suffer. During this time, I learned more about Padre Pio and the miracles that he performed, even after his death. The night before his next doctor's appointment, my father had a dream. In his dream, he was at the doctor's office. On the monitor appeared two images of Padre Pio's face where the tumor had been. After my father woke up, he felt secure that all would be well. A few days later we got the joyous news that my father was cancer-free. My parents are planning to go on a pilgrimage to Padre Pio's monastery to thank him for this miracle. – Maria Francia

I Touched the Sacred Relic

For about 20 years I have been a constant smoker. I have tried unsuccessfully on numerous occasions to give up this unhealthy habit. Recently my fourteen-year-old daughter became seriously ill. I requested that Padre Pio's relic, which was in our parish at the time, be brought to my house so that my daughter might be able to touch it. On that occasion I too managed to touch the sacred relic and since that time I have not had the urge to smoke. My daughter is well on the road to recovery. – Mrs. A. C. Patton

A Very Important Day

I recently had a very vivid dream in which I was walking with a man who was carrying a lantern. He was limping slightly as he walked and his posture was somewhat bent. He had a serious demeanor and I noticed that he seemed to be in a hurry. He spoke to me in Italian and said that a very important day was coming soon. I understood the Italian words in my dream even though I do not speak the language. Then the dream ended. I told my good friend Tony Fajardo about the dream and he then showed me a picture of Padre Pio. There was no doubt about it. He was the man I had seen in my dream. I knew practically nothing about Padre Pio. Tony had told me on a previous occasion that he had the stigmata. That was the extent of my knowledge. I had never seen a photo of Padre Pio before. I did not even know that he was from Italy. In my dream, I felt that Padre Pio was proud of me for finally realizing that the Catholic faith was destined to be a part of my life. This month I am going to begin to take classes so that I can be confirmed. In the dream, when Padre Pio said that an important date was coming up, I thought that he might be talking about his birthday. But since then, I have learned that he received the Stigmata on Sept 20 and that his feast day is September 23. I had the dream on September 6. – Nicholas Beattie

My **Father was Struck by Padre Pio's Clear, Intense Eyes**

My father met dear Padre Pio on the bus that goes to San Giovanni Rotondo from Foggia. My father was a friend of the Capuchin friars and he introduced himself to Padre Pio with his last name only. My father was at once struck by the young friar's clear, intense eyes. They travelled together speaking of the family and the war (that of 1915-1918). When they arrived at the town, they said goodbye to eachother and were about to part company when Padre Pio called my father by name saying, "Francesco, I look forward to seeing you with all your family at the friary." My father jumped when he heard his name since he introduced himself to Padre Pio with his last name only. He began to feel great admiration for Padre Pio. Punctually, the following morning, my father went up to the friary with my mother and us six children. – Maria Grazia Massa

I Went into a Deep Depression

For a very long time I could not sleep at night. The doctor gave me sleeping pills as well as pills for my nerves. I began taking all of them to no avail. After using valium, librium, and other prescription drugs, the medications had to be changed because, not only was I still unable to sleep, I went into a deep depression. Trying to keep my job as a college Spanish teacher was almost impossible. I heard about Padre Pio and had a desire to learn more about him. At the time, I shared the foreign language office at the college with the Italian professor. I asked him if he had heard of Padre Pio and he said he had. He brought me a book, Padre Pio the Stigmatist, which I read from cover to cover. After reading the book, I thought that I should pray for the glorification of Padre Pio each day. At the beginning, I said it many times but now I often start to say the prayer and then I fall asleep. I have never taken any of the medications again. – Name Withheld

A Special Blessing

My mother suffers from Alzheimer's disease. I had been taking her to an Alzheimer's day care center but recently I was told that my mother could no longer return. Her dementia was so severe that the administrator recommended that she be placed in a secured Alzheimer's facility in a nursing home. I looked and looked but could not find a facility that would fit my mother's needs. I became very worried. Then I prayed to Padre Pio and asked him to help me find something suitable. Right after that prayer I had a dream in which a saw a number of Catholic women caring for my mother. They all had dark hair but I could not see their faces clearly. In my dream, I took my mother's hand and we walked outside. We were in a heavenly place. The sky was a midnight blue, the most beautiful blue I had ever seen. It had a velvet-like quality and I would call it a "living sky" because it was pulsating with life. A huge round moon, like a glowing iridescent pearl was reflecting in the clear waters of a lake that we were standing in front of. A forest of emerald colored trees surrounded the lake. A waterfall cut through the trees, causing their leaves to shimmer and sparkle like diamonds. Every leaf was alive and shimmering. The intensity of the colors was such that the most beautiful place on earth would look like a wasteland in comparison. The beauty of what I was beholding almost took my breath away and I could not take my eyes from the sight. Then I woke up. Right after that, I went to visit another nursing home. When the administrator greeted me, I noticed that she was wearing a crucifix for a necklace. As she took me on a tour of the facility she mentioned to me that she was a Catholic. We passed by a large room where many of the residents were gathered. They were singing. They all looked happy and I also noticed that the staff was very friendly. This care home was not depressing like the others I had seen but was actually uplifting. The administrator explained to me that the Alzheimer's unit had no openings. There were 275 residents in the skilled nursing section and 50 in the Alzheimer's section and there was always a waiting list of people in the skilled nursing area waiting to move over to the Alzheimer's unit. They always had preference over anyone coming in from the outside. She took me to the Alzheimer's unit and introduced me to the head of Staff Development. She was a wonderful Catholic woman I had known a number of years ago. She told me there were no openings in the Alzheimer's unit. It was such a loving and caring environment that I decided to have my mother's name added to the waiting list even though it looked like it would be a long wait. But the problem was that I could not wait. I needed to find a place for my mother immediately. Then I went to see the Admission's administrator. As we talked, I learned that she was a member of my parish, even though I had never met her before. She told there were no openings. I told her that I had been praying to Padre Pio for my mother's needs. She seemed so surprised to hear me mention Padre Pio's name. She told me that for the first time ever, she had just sent his prayers to one of her sick relatives."I think you and I have some kind of Padre Pio connection" she said to me. Then I remembered my dream. In a very short period of time, I had just met three Catholic women and they all had dark hair, although in my dream I could not see their faces clearly. She made a short phone call and then said to me, "We do have an opening. There is one opening in the Alzheimer's unit." My mother was admitted immediately. She went to the unit for lunch and then to take a nap. My mother has been truly happy in this nursing home and the tender loving care she receives is an inspiration. Sometimes I become very sad when I remember the way my mother used to be and all that Alzheimer's disease had taken from her. Then I think about my dream and that heavenly place we were standing in. Perhaps I got a little glimpse of the beautiful place that God is preparing for my mother, when she leaves this life for a better one. Even if we have to endure many sufferings here below, it doesn't really matter so much, when we think about our true home, Heaven. – Diane Allen

I Prayed That my Son's Life Would Be Spared

The following testimony was written by a man in England (name withheld) who learned a valuable lesson regarding the sanctity of life. When he discovered that his wife was expecting their fifth child, he reacted in a spiteful way. But he eventually came to realize that each child is a gift from God and a true blessing: I am married to a wonderful and devout Catholic woman. We have four children and my wife has always made sure that our children have received a good religious education. I stopped going to Mass more than ten years ago. I was shocked when my wife told me she was expecting our fifth child. I did not want the baby and I was angry. When my wife gave birth to a baby boy, Stephen, I shrugged it off. As far as I was concerned, it was just another mouth to feed. But it was soon apparent that something was seriously wrong. Tests revealed that our son's kidneys were completely useless. One was not even a kidney at all but "mush" as the doctor called it. My heart went out to our little boy. All day long, his body jerked in pain. The doctors operated and took the "mush" away and then discovered that his other kidney was badly damaged and the tissues were dead. They told us there was no hope. Stephen's eyes were sunken and he looked like a skeleton. The ward sister and the doctors told us it was just a matter of time. They advised us to take him home from the hospital so that he could die at home surrounded by his family. I broke down when the doctor was talking to us and I suddenly had a desire to go to church and make my confession. In the confessional, I was very repentant. Around that time, I saw a book in a Catholic book shop on Padre Pio and purchased it. I read it from cover to cover. When Stephen came home from the hospital, he ate nothing, drank nothing and grew weaker by the day. His eyes stared listlessly. After two weeks at home, we saw that the end was imminent. We couldn't watch our baby die. We hurried to the hospital with him. The hospital staff said that he would probably not live through the night. I prayed and prayed to Padre Pio and to our Blessed Mother. I swore that I would never leave my faith again if my son's life was spared. I cut out a picture of Padre Pio from the book I had read and slipped it under Stephen's pillow in the hospital. He did not die that night. Each day he lingered and I continued to pray, day after day. One night I woke up. It was dark outside. Our bedroom was saturated with the perfume of roses. The aroma was over powering. The next day the doctor informed us that there was an improvement in Stephen's blood. His kidneys were working. Days turned into weeks. The doctors were amazed. They are still amazed. Stephen is now six years old. Stephen has brought so much happiness into our lives. He is my pride and joy. I have not faltered in my faith and I attend Mass each Sunday. I still say my novena to Padre Pio every day. So really there were two miracles, a miracle for Stephen and a miracle for me. My heart was once hard but it is no longer hard.

***

Padre Pio's simple cell in the monastery at San Giovanni Rotondo

St. Padre Pio on Listening to Your Guardian Angel

Padre Pio had encounters with angels throughout his life and got to know them very well. He also received interior locutions; he had to discern from whom they came and how he ought to react to them.

In a letter he wrote on July 15, 1913, to a lady named Anita, he gives her (and us) invaluable advice regarding how to act in relation to our guardian angel, locutions, and prayer.

Dear daughter of Jesus,

May your heart always be a temple of the Holy Spirit. May Jesus increase the fire of his love in your soul and may he always smile upon you, as he does on all the souls that he loves. May Mary Most Holy smile upon you during all the events of your life, and abundantly make up for the absence of your earthly mother.

May your good guardian angel always watch over you, and be your guide on the rough path of life. May he always keep you in the grace of Jesus and hold you up with his hands so that you may not hurt your foot on a stone. May he protect you under his wings from all the deceits of the world, the devil and the flesh.

Have great devotion, Anita, to this beneficent angel. How consoling it is to know that we have a spirit who, from the womb to the tomb, never leaves us even for an instant, not even when we dare to sin. And this heavenly spirit guides and protects us like a friend, a brother.

But it is very consoling to know that this angel prays unceasingly for us, and offers God all of our good actions, our thoughts, and our desires, if they are pure.

Oh! For goodness' sake, don't forget this invisible companion, ever present, ever disposed to listen to us and even more ready to console us. Oh, wonderful intimacy! Oh, blessed companionship! If only we could understand it! Keep him always before your mind's eye. Remember this angel's presence often, thank him, pray to him, always keep up a good relationship. Open yourself up to him and confide your suffering to him. Be always afraid of offending the purity of his gaze. Know this, and keep it well present in your mind. He is easily offended, very sensitive. Turn to him in moments of supreme anguish and you will experience his beneficent help.

Never say that you are alone in the battle against your enemies; never say that you have no one to whom you can open your heart and confide. It would be a grave injustice to this heavenly messenger.

Regarding interior locutions, don't worry; stay calm. What you must avoid is your heart becoming attached to these locutions. Don't give them too much importance; show that you are indifferent. You should neither scorn nor love or desire such things. Always respond to these voices thus: "Jesus, if it is you who are talking to me, let me see the facts and effects of your words, that is to say, holy virtue in me."

Humble yourself before the Lord and trust in him; spend your energy, with the help of divine grace, in the practice of the virtues, and then let grace work in you as God desires. The virtues are what sanctify the soul and not supernatural phenomena.

And don't confuse yourself trying to understand which locutions come from God. If God is their author, one of the principle signs is that as soon as you hear those voices, they fill your soul with fear and confusion, but then, they leave you in a divine peace. On the contrary, when the author of the interior locutions is the enemy, they begin with a false security, followed by agitation and indescribable malaise.

I have absolutely no doubt that God is the author of the locutions, but we must be very cautious because often the enemy mixes in a great deal of his own work with them. But this should not scare you: this is a test to which even the greatest saints and most enlightened souls were subjected, and yet they were acceptable in the eyes of the Lord. You must simply be careful not to believe in these locutions too easily, above all dealing with those that are related to how you must act and what you must do. You should receive them and submit them to the judgment of your director and resign yourself to accept his decision.

Therefore, it is best to receive the locutions with great caution and humble and constant indifference. Act in this way and everything will increase your merit before the Lord. Don't worry about your soul; Jesus loves you very much. Try to correspond to this love by progressing more and more in holiness before God and men.

Pray out loud as well; the time has not yet come to abandon these prayers. Support the difficulties you experience when doing this with patience and humility. Also be ready to suffer distractions and dryness, and you must not, under any circumstances, abandon prayer and meditation. It is the Lord who wants to treat you this way for your spiritual advantage.

Forgive me if I end here. Only God knows how difficult it has been for me to write this letter. I am very sick. Pray much that the Lord may desire to free me from this body soon.

I bless you, together with the excellent Francesca. May you live and die in the arms of Jesus.

P. Pio

Canonization of St. Pio of Pietrelcina

Homily of John Paul II

Sunday, 16 June 2002

"For my yoke is easy and my burden light" (Matthew 11:30).

Jesus' words to his disciples, which we just heard, help us to understand the most important message of this solemn celebration. Indeed, in a certain sense, we can consider them as a magnificent summary of the whole life of Padre Pio of Pietrelcina, today proclaimed a saint.

The evangelical image of the "yoke" recalls the many trials that the humble Capuchin of San Giovanni Rotondo had to face. Today we contemplate in him how gentle the "yoke" of Christ is, and how truly light is his burden when it is borne with faithful love. The life and mission of Padre Pio prove that difficulties and sorrows, if accepted out of love, are transformed into a privileged way of holiness, which opens onto the horizons of a greater good, known only to the Lord.

"But may I never boast except in the cross of Our Lord Jesus Christ" (Galatians 6:14).

Is it not, precisely, the "glory of the Cross" that shines above all in Padre Pio? How timely is the spirituality of the Cross lived by the humble Capuchin of Pietrelcina. Our time needs to rediscover the value of the Cross in order to open the heart to hope.

Throughout his life, he always sought greater conformity with the Crucified, since he was very conscious of having been called to collaborate in a special way in the work of redemption. His holiness cannot be understood without this constant reference to the Cross.

In God's plan, the Cross constitutes the true instrument of salvation for the whole of humanity and the way clearly offered by the Lord to those who wish to follow him (see Mark 16:24). The Holy Franciscan of the Gargano understood this well, when on the Feast of the Assumption in 1914, he wrote: "In order to succeed in reaching our ultimate end we must follow the divine Head, who does not wish to lead the chosen soul on any way other than the one he followed; by that, I say, of abnegation and the Cross." (Epistolario II, p. 155).

"I am the Lord who acts with mercy" (Jeremiah 9:23).

Padre Pio was a generous dispenser of divine mercy, making himself available to all by welcoming them, by spiritual direction and, especially, by the administration of the sacrament of Penance. I also had the privilege, during my young years, of benefiting from his availability for penitents. The ministry of the confessional, which is one of the distinctive traits of his apostolate, attracted great crowds of the faithful to the monastery of San Giovanni Rotondo. Even when that unusual confessor treated pilgrims with apparent severity, the latter, becoming conscious of the gravity of sins and sincerely repentant, almost always came back for the peaceful embrace of sacramental forgiveness.

May his example encourage priests to carry out with joy and zeal this ministry which is so important today, as I wished to confirm this year in the Letter to Priests on the occasion of Holy Thursday.

"You, Lord, are my only good."

This is what we sang in the responsorial psalm. Through these words, the new Saint invites us to place God above everything, to consider him our sole and highest good.

In fact, the ultimate reason for the apostolic effectiveness of Padre Pio, the profound root of so much spiritual fruitfulness can be found in that intimate and constant union with God, attested to by his long hours spent in prayer and in the confessional. He loved to repeat, "I am a poor Franciscan who prays" convinced that "prayer is the best weapon we have, a key that opens the heart of God".

This fundamental characteristic of his spirituality continues in the "Prayer Groups" that he founded, which offer to the Church and to society the wonderful contribution of incessant and confident prayer. To prayer, Padre Pio joined an intense charitable activity, of which the "Home for the Relief of Suffering" is an extraordinary expression. Prayer and charity, this is the most concrete synthesis of Padre Pio's teaching, which today is offered to everyone.

"I give praise to you, Father, Lord of heaven and earth, for although you have hidden these things from the wise and the learned you have revealed them to the childlike"(Matthew 11:25).

How appropriate are these words of Jesus, when we think of them as applied to you, humble and beloved Padre Pio.

Teach us, we ask you, humility of heart, so we may be counted among the little ones of the Gospel, to whom the Father promised to reveal the mysteries of His Kingdom.

Help us to pray without ceasing, certain that God knows what we need even before we ask Him.

Obtain for us the eyes of faith that will help us recognize in the poor and suffering, the very face of Jesus.

Sustain us in the hour of trouble and trial and, if we fall, let us experience the joy of the sacrament of forgiveness.

Grant us your tender devotion to Mary, the Mother of Jesus and our Mother.

Accompany us on our earthly pilgrimage toward the blessed Homeland, where we too, hope to arrive to contemplate forever the glory of the Father, the Son and the Holy Spirit.

Amen.

John Paul II praying at Padre Pio's tomb
in San Giovanni Rotondo on May 25, 1987

Address of John Paul II – Day Following Canonization of St. Padre Pio

Monday, June 17 2002

Dear Brothers and Sisters,

It is a great joy for me to meet you again the day after the solemn canonization of the humble Capuchin of San Giovanni Rotondo. Dear pilgrims and devotees, I greet you with affection who have gathered in Rome in such large numbers for this special occasion. I first of all greet the bishops, priests and religious who are present here. I want to pay special attention to the Capuchin Franciscans who in communion with the whole Church praise and thank the Lord for the marvels he has worked in their exemplary confrere. Padre Pio is an authentic model of spirituality and humanity, two characteristic features of the Franciscan and Capuchin tradition.

I greet the members of the "Padre Pio Prayer Groups" and the representatives of the family of the "Home for the Relief of Suffering," that great institution for the treatment and the care of the sick that came forth from the new saint's charity. I embrace you, dear pilgrims from the noble land that gave birth to Padre Pio, from the other regions of Italy and from every part of the world. By your presence here, you witness to how widespread is devotion to and confidence in the holy Friar of the Gargano in the Church and on every continent.

But what is the secret of such great admiration and love for this new saint? He is first of all a "friar of the people," a traditional characteristic of the Capuchins. He is also a saint who is a miraculous healer, as the extraordinary events which are part of his life attest. However, above all, Padre Pio is a religious who is deeply in love with the crucified Christ. He even shared physically in the mystery of the Cross during his life.

He liked to link the glory of Tabor with the mystery of the Passion, as we read in one of his letters: "Before exclaiming with St. Peter, "Oh how good it is to be here," it is necessary first to climb Calvary, where one sees only death, nails, thorns, suffering, extraordinary shadows, abandonment and fainting" (Epistolario III).

Padre Pio made his journey of demanding spiritual ascesis in communion with the Church. The temporary misunderstandings he had with one or other ecclesial authority did not put a brake on his attitude of filial obedience. Padre Pio was a faithful and courageous son of the Church and in this situation he followed the shining example of the "Poverello" of Assisi.

May this holy Capuchin to whom so many people turn to from every corner of the earth point out to us the means to reach holiness which is the goal of our life as Christians. How many faithful in every social condition, from the most diverse places and the most difficult situations hurried to ask his help. He knew how to offer them all what they needed most, which they were often groping for without being fully aware of it. He passed on to them the comforting and enlightening Word of God, enabling each person to draw from the sources of his grace through his diligent dedication to the ministry of the confessional and the fervent celebration of the Eucharist. So it was that he wrote to one of his spiritual daughters, "Do not be afraid to come to the Lord's altar to be fed with flesh of the Immaculate Lamb, because no one will better reconcile your spirit than your King, nothing will warm it more than His sun, and nothing will soothe it better than His balm."

The Mass of Padre Pio. It was an eloquent reminder to priests of the beauty of the priestly vocation. For the religious and the lay people who flocked to San Giovanni Rotondo even at the early morning hours, it was an extraordinary catechesis on the value and importance of the Eucharistic sacrifice.

Holy Mass was the heart and the source of his whole spirituality: "There is in the Mass," he used to say, "the whole of Calvary." The faithful who crowded round his altar were profoundly impressed by the intensity of his "immersion" in the Mystery, and perceived that "the Father" participated in his person in the Redeemer's sufferings.

St Pio of Pietrelcina presented himself to everyone – priests, men and women religious and lay people – as a credible witness to Christ and to his Gospel. May his example and intercession spur everyone to greater love for God and concrete solidarity with his neighbor, especially those who are in greatest need.

May the Blessed Virgin Mary, whom Padre Pio called by the beautiful name of "Our Lady of Grace" (Santa Maria delle Grazie), help us to follow in the footprints of this religious who is so beloved by the people.

With this hope, I cordially bless you who are present here, your loved ones and all who are committed to following in the spiritual footsteps of the beloved saint of Pietrelcina.

– *Pope John Paul II*

41794852R00056

Printed in Poland
by Amazon Fulfillment
Poland Sp. z o.o., Wrocław